Windows on the World

Plays and Activities Adapted from Folk Tales from Different Lands

Written by Sylvia Sikundar
Illustrated by Diane Williams

Pacific Educational Press
Vancouver Canada

Published by Pacific Educational Press
Faculty of Education
University of British Columbia
Vancouver, B.C. V6T 1Z4
Telephone: (604) 822-5385
Fax: (604) 822-6603

The publisher would like to acknowledge the assistance of Heritage Canada with the development of its publishing program. Our thanks also go to Sean Chew, from Burnaby South Secondary School, for help scanning the illustrations in this book.

Canadian Cataloguing in Publication Data

Sikundar Sylvia, 1945-
  Windows on the world

  ISBN 0-88865-089-2

  1. College and school drama. 2. Folklore--Juvenile drama.
I. Williams, Diane, 1955- . II. Title
PS8587.I48W56 1994   j812'.54   C94-910258X
PR9199.3.S54W56 1994

Edited by: Janis Barr and Carolyn Sale
Cover design: Warren Clark
Cover art and inside illustrations: Diane Williams

Printed in Canada
9 8 7 6 5 4 3 2 1

Contents

Introduction

This book contains five original plays based on folk tales from five different cultures: the Celtic traditions of Scotland, the aboriginal culture of Australia, and the folk cultures of Indonesia, Korea, and India. The plays are the book's core. Their scripts have been designed for use with children 10-13 years of age, but they can easily be adapted for use with younger and older children.

This book is divided into five parts, one for each play. Each chapter begins with a short text that introduces the play and the culture it is from, along with relevant background information. The play script is then provided on reproducible masters along with patterns for masks and other costume elements. Each chapter provides suggestions for staging the play, specific instructions for the decoration of masks and costumes, and suggestions for props and the construction of scenery. Included in these suggestions are ideas for drawing upon some of the culture's artistic traditions when designing sets and props.

Appended to each chapter is an activities section, which suggests a number of ways in which your group can explore the geography, music, history, art, and social customs of the culture of the play. The activities encourage hands-on, tactile experiments with the fine arts of the five cultures, as well as other dramatic approaches, a further delving into the folk tales of the culture, language games, and suggestions for research into the topography, animal life, history, and religious beliefs of these cultures. Many of these activities are open-ended to allow you as parent, educator, or community group leader to adapt them to the needs and the curiosities of the children with whom you are working. Some also suggest ways in which members of your group can share their talents, knowledge, and cultural backgrounds with others.

Many activities provide background information about various aspects of the plays' cultures. You may wish to read the activities for information that may be helpful in the performances.

Folk Tales and Myths

Folk tales offer a particularly imaginative and expansive way into a study of the world's cultures. They are windows into the lives and beliefs of societies around the planet. They are also windows into the past, and are an invitation to do a kind of time travelling. Through them we can learn about both contemporary and ancient cultures. Across geographical and chronological distances, we can discover aspects of human lives that have remained unchanged—stories embodying ideas and values that have endured across centuries and that have travelled with peoples as they have migrated from place to place.

Some of the stories are myths. Myths preserve beliefs about the origins of humanity, various life forms, and geographical wonders, and they have helped cultures establish and understand their interaction with the spirit world and the environment. Often in myths magical transformations occur—men and women become animals and birds, and birds and animals become humans—and this magical element is often found in folk tales as well. Folk tales have a different emphasis, however; they focus on relationships between humans and have functioned historically as an important means by which a society establishes its moral codes. Both myths and folk tales have been passed down through two of the oldest forms of human communication, the arts of story telling and drama. These are the principal means by which any culture transmits its values, beliefs, and practices from generation to generation.

Drama

Drama is experiential, active learning. Drama can help children interpret and make sense of their own world and the worlds of others. It helps develop imagination and empathy, and provides opportunities for children to explore the thoughts, feelings, and actions of others through interaction and reflection. Drama is, by its nature, a cooperative venture. It helps children develop creative and critical abilities as well as communication skills through talking, planning, improvising, role-playing, problem-solving, and group decision-making.

Masks

Each play includes mask patterns for the characters in the play. Masks play a vital role in effecting the magical interplay between the "real" and the "fabulous" or spiritual so often found in myths and folk tales. A mask is a talisman. Lying on a table or put away in a trunk, it is inert, lifeless; but many cultures believe that when a sacred mask is donned, it transforms the wearer into the spirit that it embodies. It may be difficult to communicate to children the powerful ritualistic role that masks play in many cultures, but the fun of preparing and donning their masks will let the children in your group participate in the wonder of transformation that the masks facilitate. Young performers generally enjoy wearing masks—the masks liberate them from their inhibitions and help them get more fully "into character." The masks also give the children in your group the chance to look at the world from another vantage point—literally through other eyes!—to help them broaden their perspectives on the world.

Options for Staging the Plays

Plays can be performed in a variety of ways. Three of these—full productions, staged readings, and puppet plays—are described here. You might also consider improvisations, radio plays, films (video), pantomimes, or choral readings.

A Full Production

If you choose to stage a full-fledged production of one of the plays, complete with costumes, masks, scenery, and music, every member of your group, no matter how shy they may be, can contribute in a significant way to the production. Children who have no desire to perform can contribute other talents. For example, non-performers can act as the art crew. As such they will be responsible for coordinating the production of scenery and costumes. They can also perform the roles of stage manager and technicians, taking responsibility for organizing the stage, making sure props are where they ought to be, playing music where appropriate, and orchestrating any other technical effects included in your production. Almost all of the plays involve a potentially limitless number of non-speaking roles so that every member of your group can have the fun of preparing a mask. Information about making masks is in the section on scenery, costumes, and music below.

Actors should be encouraged to memorize their lines, but a prompter and/or cue cards can be used to bolster student confidence. For younger children who may not be up to the challenge of memorization, another dramatic tradition, that of mime, can be drawn upon. One child can mime the part, while another, script in hand, reads it.

During rehearsal, every member of your group can take part in the directorial role. Each member can provide suggestions for how performers should talk, move, and gesture, can contribute ideas about what music should be used and when, and can help decide how particular important movements should be choreographed.

Staged Readings (Reader's Theatre)

Staged readings offer your group another way of performing the plays if you do not have the time or resources to mount a full production. In a staged reading, lines are not memorized, but read from scripts. Performers sit on chairs or stools throughout the reading, and rise only to perform essential actions. Masks can still be used as well as key props, but backdrops or other pieces of scenery are not necessary.

Because no memorization is required, performers can concentrate on understanding the play and delivering dialogue with greater attention to its meaning. For a group of children where the majority want speaking parts, you could break into smaller groups with each group preparing a staged reading of a different play in the book.

Puppet Plays

Your group could produce a version of one of this book's plays in another way—as a puppet play. With this approach, memorization is not an issue since lines can be read or improvised. If you are interested in pursuing this option, please see the discussion of puppet plays in "The Tiger's Whisker" and "The Hare's Liver."

Suggestions for a Full Production

Detailed suggestions for staging each play are found in each chapter. The following are performance and production considerations that apply to all the plays.

The Performance Area

Plays are conventionally performed in one of two different types of spaces. Plays can be performed on a stage, behind what is called a proscenium arch. In western society, this has been the most common way of presenting plays since the late seventeenth century. Plays can also be performed "in the round"—in any space where the audience can surround the action in a horseshoe or a complete circle. Theatre in the round is the way in which most of the cultures represented in this book present their masked dramas, and often that performance space is outdoors. All three possibilities—a stage or an open space either indoors or outdoors—are suitable for the plays in this book. If you have access to both types of spaces, you may want to keep in mind that theatre in the round encourages greater interaction between the performers and the audience, and with many of the plays in this book, such an interaction will add to the liveliness and the humour of your production. Whatever you decide, your choice of playing area will affect movement possibilities as well as your need for scenery, so select your playing area before making any other design or performance decisions.

Scenery, Props, Costumes, and Music

Art and music are central to the development and expression of cultural identities as well as enhancing a play production. By producing their masks, children will have a chance to try their hand at different art traditions while creating their own personal and unique images. Designing backdrops and other scenery will also allow your group to make use of the art traditions of the culture from which the play is drawn. Choosing and recording music is another way to explore an aspect of the play's culture.

Suggestions specific to each play can be found in each chapter. The following are general suggestions applicable to all the plays.

Scenery

Scenery may include individual objects (trees and rocks, for example) and/or a backdrop (such as a mural or other artworks). If the play is to be performed outdoors, natural objects can provide the scenery.

Some children may also act as scenery by dressing appropriately. More than one play in this book requires some non-speaking performers to represent scenery elements. For other plays, some children may want to add tree or plant parts and participate in the production. This may help those students who don't feel ready to act feel more comfortable being on stage.

Props

Props can be found or made. Your art crew should read the script carefully to find mention of any props needed by the characters in the play. Encourage them to think of other props not specifically mentioned that might enhance the production of the play and help the actors develop their characters more fully.

Wherever possible, symbols or design motifs from the play's culture should be incorporated into the design of these props. Information about the symbols of each culture is included with each play, but the members of your art crew could research these further on their own.

Encourage your art crew to keep the nature of the "fabulous" in mind when they are designing the scenery and the props for their play. Vivid colours, for example, and larger than life sizes will emphasize the mythic nature of the plays—and add to their humour in performance!

Costumes

Each play in this book includes pattern masters for masks and other costume elements for the characters. Although the plays can be performed without masks, their use greatly enhances the performances.

The mask patterns in this book are in reproducible form and may be photocopied directly onto paper or cardboard. You may wish to laminate the patterns to make permanent masters. Masks can also be laminated after they have been decorated and before they are assembled, so that they can be used in art displays. You may need to enlarge or reduce the masks to fit individual members of your group. This can be done on a photocopier set to an appropriate percentage.

Encourage members of your group to be as creative as possible in the creation of their masks. Assure them that in productions that involve more than one of a particular animal, there is no need for these animals to be identical in their colouring or any other aspect. Suggestions to help children explore the emotional impact of colour, monochromatic colour schemes, simulation of textured surfaces, and other art techniques are included with the plays.

Following are general assembly instructions applicable to all the masks in this book. For masks that require special assembly, detailed instructions are provided with the plays. For some plays, additional costumes are required. Suggestions for these are provided as needed.

1. Complete all costume decorations before cutting out the pattern pieces for assembly.
2. Cut out the mask and other costume pieces along the heavy black lines. Also cut the heavy black lines within the pieces to create holes for eyes or nostrils, or to help a nose or an ear pop out to create a three-dimensional effect. These dark lines also indicate where tabs of other pieces will be inserted.
3. Two dots connected by a line (●━━━●) indicate a fold line. Fold along these lines before any gluing or inserting.
4. The masks are assembled using both glue and tape. A tab with an arrow (→) means that the tab should be inserted through a slot and taped on the back of the mask. Corresponding letters indicate where to insert the tab (A, A). Diagonal lines (▨) show where glue is placed. Diagonal lines on a tab mean the tab should be folded, then glued in place. Corresponding letters show where to glue two pieces together (A, A). Join the two halves of the breastplates together by gluing along the vertical glue line.
5. To wear the masks and breastplates, ties must be added. Punch out the heavy black circles with a hole punch and tie thread or string through each hole. Tie on the masks or breastplates.

Music

Music can greatly enhance a performance, whether it is a full production, a staged reading, or a puppet play. Music can be used to set the mood at the beginning, as a dramatic finale, and within the play to facilitate scene changes or to heighten the effect of particular scenes. Music should never be allowed to detract from the play's dialogue, however. Suggestions for music accompany each play.

You may use recorded music for educational purposes without permission. But permission must be obtained to use music in performances open to the public. See the copyright page for information about obtaining permission.

A Cultural Note

A single tale—or a play written from such a tale—cannot possibly hope to capture fully any culture's complexity and infinite variety. India alone, for example, has over 100 languages currently in use, each representing a subculture with its own stories and traditions. The premise of this book is that a single tale does have something very particular to offer, however—a glimpse into another culture. We hope that this glimpse will inspire children to further explorations into the riches of other cultures and that these investigations will enhance their appreciation of the diversity and wonder of life on this planet. We also hope that through performing these plays, children will begin to see the similarities that connect cultures, and through their explorations will find the common threads that bind us all together.

The Wounded Seal

About the Play

"The Wounded Seal" tells the story of an encounter between a seal hunter and a group of seals that causes the hunter to rethink his occupation. It is based on a well known folk tale told by the fishing people of western Scotland and the offshore islands which are known as the Western Isles.

This folk tale is about the seal people (called *selchies* or *silkies*), gentle beings who do no harm unless provoked. They are thought to have the ability to transform themselves into humans. People who drown at sea are thought by some to have joined the *selchies*. It is considered very unlucky to harm a seal and many people are reluctant to do so. In one version of this folk tale, the *selchies* are believed to be members of the clan MacCodrum, of whom there are no living descendants in the Western Isles. It is believed that the MacCodrums were turned into *selchies* because one of them killed a cuckoo, a bird special to and protected by the fairies.

In the play, the Stranger—who is really a *selchie*—uses a seal cape to transform the main character, Angus, into a seal so that Angus can accompany him to the seals' home at the bottom of the sea. Transformation into an animal by donning its skin is a very common element in folk tales. Belief in such a transformation was very important to the Celts, whose Druidic priests wore capes made of bird feathers to access the magical powers they attributed to birds.

It is believed that the first Celtic migration to Scotland took place over two thousand years ago in the first century B.C.E.* when a tribe called the Picts crossed to Scotland from the continent of Europe. Some of these Celts went to Ireland. In the third or fourth century C.E.,* a tribe of these Celts called Scots returned from Ireland, and it is from this tribe that Scotland gets its modern name. The Picts and the Scots battled for power in Scotland for centuries. The rugged nature of Scotland's terrain made it less accessible to other invaders, and it was never occupied by the Romans, although Julius Caesar subdued the Celts in most of Europe and elsewhere in Britain. Descendants of the battling Picts and Scots still live in parts of Ireland and Scotland and the islands in between from which this play's folk tale is drawn—among them, Lewis, Skye, Mull, and Kintyre. One can still find aspects of the Celtic heritage in the traditions of western Scotland that have survived for almost two thousand years.

If you would like to know more about the Celts, their legends, and their relationships with the animal world, you may find the following books useful:

Cunliffe, Barry. *The Celtic World.* London: The Bodley Head, 1979.

Delaney, Frank. *Legends of the Celts.* London: Hodder & Stoughton, 1985.

Green, Miranda. *Animals in Celtic Life and Myth.* London and New York: Routledge, 1992.

———. *Celtic Myths.* Austin: University of Texas Press, 1993.

Jacobs, Joseph. *Celtic Fairy Tales.* New York and London: G.P. Putnam, 1923.

Norton, Duncan, et al. *The Celts.* N.p., 1974.

Ross, Ann. *Everyday Life of the Pagan Celts.* London, New York, Batsford: G.P. Putnam, 1970.

Thomasen, David. *The People of the Sea.* London: Barrie & Rockcliff, 1985.

Williamson, Duncan. *The Broonie, Silkies and Fairies. Travellers' Tales of Other Worlds.* New York: Harmony Books, 1985.

---

* before the Christian era and the Christian era itself, respectively.

Suggestions for Performing the Play

General information on play performance can be found on pages 5-7. "The Wounded Seal" takes approximately 8 minutes to perform. The play has 10 speaking parts, although other students can play non-speaking seals if you would like to include a greater number of students in the performance. Students could also extend the number of speaking parts by writing extra dialogue to incorporate into the play.

If the play is performed on a stage, the initial exchanges between Angus, Robbie, and Alistair, and then Angus and the Stranger could take place in front of a dropped curtain that could later be raised to reveal the underwater scene. If you are using an open playing area, you could have a large cluster of rocks in the centre of the playing space. One side of the rocks could be designated as the seashore and the seals could watch Angus, Alistair, and Robbie from the other side. When Angus is busy counting his pelts, the Stranger could rise from the rocks, remove his mask and seal cape, and approach Angus. When it is time for Angus to be transformed into a seal so he can accompany the Stranger on his journey, the seals could rise from the rocks and surround Angus to drape him in his seal cape and put on his seal mask. One or two of the seals could bring the Stranger his cape and mask so that he, too, can become a seal again.

The journey into the sea can be represented in a number of ways. One suggestion is to have the seals rise from the rocks in pairs. Each pair of seals would have a roll of blue or green paper or a length of blue or green cloth that would be unwound as the seals circle around the Stranger and Angus to represent a whirlwind descent to the bottom of the ocean. As they arrive at their destination, the seals would wind the ribbon or material into rolls again and tuck the rolls out of the audience's sight.

For the second scene, the cluster of rocks should be moved fairly close to the audience to ensure that the Seal Father can be seen and heard, despite his prone position. For dramatic effect, the rest of the seal family must keep the Seal Father hidden from view until it is time for the Stranger to introduce him to Angus. Likewise, the knife should not be seen until it is time for the Stranger to present it to Angus. One of the seals could give the knife to the Stranger at the appropriate time.

Encourage your group to decide for themselves how they would like to represent the crying of the seals. Have them keep in mind that their cries must not overwhelm the spoken dialogue.

Suggestions for Scenery, Props, Costumes, and Music

Scenery

The play has two settings, one on land and one at the bottom of the sea. If your group wants to create a backdrop, the backdrop for both settings could show the land scene to help establish the play's physical setting. The coastline of northwest Scotland is greatly affected by fierce winds off the Atlantic and is dominated by cliffs (which are called *braes* in Gaelic). Glens—narrow, steep-sided valleys—often descend to the sea where the waters of the Atlantic meet it in a sea *loch* (lake). The moors on top of the cliffs are often studded with heather. Your group could consult photographs of the braes and glens of Scotland to create their backdrop in greys and greens and heather-purple.

At the centre of the playing space, as described in the previous section, you will need a large rock cluster. Crumpled newspapers could be shaped and glued into rock-like shapes. For sturdier rocks you could use papier mâché. You could colour the rocks by coating the newspaper with a grey tempera wash.

Props

A performance of "The Wounded Seal" requires three important props: seal pelts, a wound for the seal father, and Angus's fishing knife.

To make the seal pelts that Angus carries, your art crew could draw the outline of a seal pelt onto newspaper and cut out two copies for each seal pelt they wish to make. One copy could be painted with a grey-brown tempera wash. Then the two shapes could be stapled together, leaving an opening for stuffing the pelt. The pelt could be stuffed with a thin layer of crumpled paper and the opening stapled shut. Strips of brown and black wool could be pasted onto the painted pelt forms and shellacked with Rhoplex® to simulate the dark, oily texture of a seal's coat. A pattern for a seal pelt is provided below that can be enlarged to a realistic size. Since Angus is an accomplished hunter and has just returned from a very successful day's hunting, your group will want to make quite a few pelts for him to carry.

The wound on the seal father may be made from a piece of red tissue paper glued to a circle of slightly heavier paper. The wound should be taped lightly to the seal father's back so that Angus can remove it easily and crumple it in his hand when he heals the seal father.

The prop knife can be made from cardboard and paper painted silver and red for the seal father's dried blood. The hilt of the knife could be decorated with a Celtic knot or with a design of an animal important in Celtic culture.

Costumes

General instructions for mask and breastplate decoration and construction can be found on page 7. For this play, Celtic knots have been incorporated into the mask and breastplate design. Here are specific instructions for this play's masks and breastplates.

Seal Costumes

To decorate the seal masks and breastplates, use pencil or wax crayons in browns, greys, silvers, blues, purples, and white. To create a textured fur-like effect, layer colours like grey, silver, white, and a pale blue on top of each other, or layer different shades of blue and purple. To achieve a light and dark effect, vary the pressure you apply to your crayon or pencil.

When constructing the masks, be sure to cut the eyebrow lines to help give the mask a three-dimensional effect. The seal nose has 4 fold lines. Fold all of these *before* inserting tab A into slot A and gluing tab B to spot B. Glue the seal's whiskers to the appropriate spots (C and D).

Music

Music can help establish a pace for Angus's transformation and journey as well as contribute to the magic of it. Harp music or a Celtic folk song would be a good choice. If you wish, you can also use music such as bagpipe music to establish the mood and the cultural background of the play before it starts.

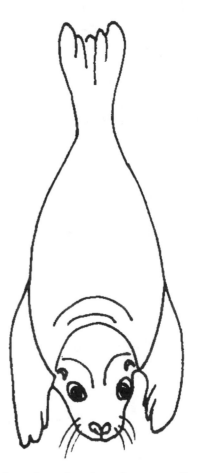

This drawing can be enlarged and used as an outline to make seal pelts for Angus to carry over his shoulder.

The Wounded Seal

Robbie and Alistair enter from one direction, Angus from the other.

Robbie: Good day, Angus. Have you had a good day's hunting?

Angus: I've had a marvellous day, thanks, Robbie, thanks, Alistair.

(Angus turns his back to Robbie and Alistair and then to the audience. His back is covered in seal pelts.)

Alistair: So many? It's no wonder you're such a famous hunter.

Angus: I'm going to get a good price for these. And I've already thought of several ways I can spend the money.

Robbie *(chuckling)*: I'm sure you have.

Alistair: You had better hope that there were no selchies among that lot you caught today, Angus.

Angus: Selchies! You must be joking! You don't believe that old story, do you? About seals who transform themselves into human beings?

Robbie: Of course we believe it!

Alistair: Our great-grandfather was one of the finest seal hunters this island has ever seen.

Robbie: Until he met a selchie.

Alistair: After he met a selchie, all he did for the rest of his days was cut peat.

Robbie: That's right. And he spent the rest of his life telling everyone who would listen about the time he met the selchies. He never hunted another seal again as long as he lived.

Alistair: And he told our grandfather the story —

Robbie: And our grandfather told our father —

Alistair: And our father told us.

Robbie: And our family has been peat cutters ever since.

Angus: You MacLeod boys make me laugh! That was just a story to entertain you on long, cold winter evenings.

Alistair: You believe that if you want to, Angus. But you'll meet a selchie one day.

Alistair and Robbie exit laughing.

Angus: What do a pair of silly old peat cutters know about the sea? Selchies! What nonsense!

Angus counts his pelts. He has already counted them several times, but he can't resist the desire to count them again. While he is busy counting, a Stranger enters.

Stranger: Good evening, sir!

Angus: Good evening.

Stranger: You're Angus MacLean, aren't you?

Angus: Yes, that's right. Who are you?

Stranger: It doesn't matter who I am. I've heard about your reputation as a seal hunter. It looks as if you've had a particularly good day today.

Angus: I sure have.

Stranger: Well, Angus, I know someone who would like to buy as many pelts as possible tonight. If you like, I can take you to him, but you must come right away. He's a stranger to these parts and he's leaving first thing in the morning.

Angus: Well, you've come to the right man. How many does he want?

Stranger: I don't know. You'll have to speak with him yourself. Come with me, and I'll take you straight to him. He's spending the night with a friend who lives by the sea.

Angus: Well, let's go then. I don't mind doing a quick bit of business before supper.

The Stranger takes Angus by the arm.

Stranger: This way, Angus. Across the moor.

Angus: Are you sure? I don't think anyone lives in this direction. The MacCodrums lived here once, but their house is empty now. Do you know what people say happened to them? They say the fairies turned them into seals.

Stranger: Yes, Angus, I know.

Angus: Really? How would you have heard the story?

Stranger: I'm a MacCodrum, Angus.

Angus: You're a —? I'm sorry. I don't understand.

Stranger: You will, Angus, you will. I'm going to help you understand. I'm going to take you on a journey. And to do that I'm going to have to turn you into one of us.

Angus: One of you? What are you talking about?

Seals surround Angus and place the seal skin cape around his shoulders. The Stranger puts on a seal mask and a cape.

Angus: Hey! What are you doing?

Stranger: We are taking you to our home in the sea.

Angus: Your home in the sea! Where is the man who was just here with me? What have you done with him?

Stranger: I was that man. I'm a selchie. I'm a seal when I'm in the water and a man when I'm on land.

Angus: A selchie! You must be joking! Robbie and Alistair put you up to this, didn't they?

Stranger: This is no joke, Angus.

They plunge into the sea. They arrive at the home of the seals where several seals are crying.

Angus: Oh, dear. What a terrible racket! Why are they so unhappy?

Stranger: You should know, Angus.

Angus *(putting his arm around Seal 1):* Cheer up, my friend. What on earth could be so terrible? Why are you crying?

Seal 1: Today my children went out to play on the rocks, and they haven't returned.

Angus: Well, don't give up hope. Maybe they'll come home later.

Seal 1: No, Angus, they're gone forever. You should know that.

Angus *(to Seal 2):* Oh, please stop crying. You're making me cry, too. Why are you crying?

Seal 2: Today my grandparents went to lie in the sun, but they haven't returned.

Angus *(to Seals 3 and 4 who are huddled together):* Did you lose someone too?

Seals 3 and **4** *(together):* Our mother went to get us some fish, but she hasn't come home.

Stranger: Why do you look so surprised, Angus? Surely you knew that when you killed a seal you killed someone's mother or daughter or son.

Angus: But I'd never thought of it that way!

Stranger: Do you recognize this?

The Stranger holds up a fishing knife. Angus takes a frightened step backwards.

Seal 5: There's no reason for you to be frightened, Angus. We are peaceful creatures. We wouldn't think of hurting you.

Seal 1: That's right, Angus. We won't hurt you. We just want to know the truth.

Angus: I'll tell you the truth. Yes, I recognize that

knife. It's mine. I lost it today. I plunged it into a really large seal, but he was a fighter. He wouldn't give up. He almost pulled me out of my boat he was struggling so hard. He got away from me with my knife still in his back.

Stranger: Angus, that seal was my father. He managed to make it home to us, but he is badly wounded. Your knife was sticking in his back when he came home. We had to pull it free.

Angus: Oh, my! This is *so* horrible. I'm sorry! I had no idea …

Stranger: Because you are the one who harmed him, you are the only one who can help him. If you lay your hands over his wound with genuine sorrow for what you have done, he will recover.

Angus: Well, take me to him. I'll do what I can.

The Stranger takes Angus to the place where his father is lying groaning.

Stranger: See where the wound is? Put your hands on it.

Angus places his hands over the Seal Father's wound. The Seal Father's groans become less violent.

Seal 2: He's getting better.

Seal 5: You must be truly sorry, Angus.

Angus: I am! I am!

Seals 3 and 4: Look! He's sitting up!

Seal Father: Thank you for giving me back my life, Angus.

Stranger: You'll get strong again, Father. I know you will.

Seal Father: Yes, and if I am lucky and stay away from hunters, I may live a few more years.

Angus: Oh, please forgive me. I had no idea of the sorrow I was causing. I have to confess I was only thinking of the money I earned.

Stranger: Do you truly want our forgiveness?

Angus: Oh, please! I won't be able to live with myself unless you forgive me.

Seal 5: Then you must make a promise.

Angus: Anything, anything!

Seal 5: Angus, you must promise never to harm another seal again as long as you live.

Angus: I want to promise that. I really do. But how will I make money?

Stranger: There are other ways to make money, Angus.

Angus: Yes, that's true. I could raise sheep or dye wool or cut peat like Alistair and Robbie. I'm young. I can learn to do something other than hunt for seals.

Seal 5: So you promise, then?

Angus: Oh, yes. I promise. I'll never harm a seal or any other creature again. And I'll tell everyone I know about my meeting with you so that no one else in the village will hunt seals either.

Seal Father: I am so glad to hear that, Angus. Every time you look out to sea you will know that the ocean is filled with your friends.

Angus: Yes, I will. I will always remember you.

Stranger: Come, Angus. Let me take you home.

Seal Breastplate and Whiskers

Seal Breastplate and Whiskers

Activities

Designing an Illuminated Letter
Background Information

The Celts were great warriors and charioteers, but they were also talented metal workers and artists. They fashioned ornaments in bronze to decorate their homes, weaponry, and clothes including bowls and flagons, necklaces and bracelets, harnesses for their horses, and brooches for their cloaks. The pagan Celt belief that boundaries between the human and the animal worlds were not fixed is reflected in the artistic design of these objects, which often blend an animal and a human into a single figure. The pagan Celts also believed that some animals—the pig, the bull, and the salmon, for example—were sacred. A brooch might contain a sacred bird or animal in its design to endow it with magical powers.

In the fifth century C.E., after the Romans left Britain, some Celts became Christians, and monks established monasteries in isolated coastal areas and on small islands. Here the Celts' love of art was put to use in book manuscripts that the Celts decorated with intricate patterns, continuing the Celtic tradition of melding animal and human forms. The illustrations for these hand written texts were brightly coloured and sometimes embellished with gold or silver. They lit up the pages—which is how the books got their name of illuminated manuscripts. Illuminated manuscripts were produced by monks throughout Europe for centuries, but many of the Celtic manuscripts are considered artistic masterpieces. The most famous of these are *The Book of Kells* and *The Lindisfarne Gospels.* Unfortunately, the monasteries where many illuminated manuscripts were housed were often raided by Vikings who destroyed many of these works of art.

Activity

Your group may want to try some art techniques used by the Celts and, in particular, may enjoy drawing and decorating illuminated letters of their own. **Art Master 1** provides the letter "C" as an example.

Using a light pencil outline, combine two or more creatures—fantastical creatures like dragons or living things like snakes, birds, or fish—in the shape of a capital letter. (Each member of your group may want to use the first initial of their name.) Another small creature could either rest on top or inside the capital letter. Once the letter has been shaped, it can be decorated with Celtic knots, zigzag patterns, spirals, or floral patterns. Then the letter's outline can be traced in black and its interior coloured. To complete the design, draw a continuous line of red, black, gold, or silver dots outside of, but close to, the letter.

The following books will provide you with more information about Celtic art and manuscript illumination and the most famous of the Celtic illuminated manuscripts:

Backhouse, Janet. *The Lindisfarne Gospels.* Ithaca, NY: Cornell University Press, 1981

Davis, Courtney. *Celtic Mandalas.* London, New York, and Blandford: Sterling, 1994.

Henry, Françoise. *The Book of Kells.* N.p., 1970.

Meehan, Aiden. *Celtic Design: A Beginner's Manual.* New York: Thames & Hudson, 1992.

———. *Celtic Design: Spiral Patterns.* New York: Thames & Hudson, 1993.

———. *Knotwork: The Secret Method of the Scribes.* London: Thames & Hudson, 1991.

Investigating Celtic Holidays
Background Information

The Celts had a strong belief in the supernatural and believed that the space between things was a source of danger. Our modern holiday of Hallowe'en may have had its origin in the ancient Celtic festival of *Samain. Samain,* the Celtic new year, was celebrated on November 1st.

The Celts thought that during the night of October 31st, there was a gap between the old and the new year when the real world and the afterworld were open to each other, allowing the movement of ghosts and spirits between the two. The festival of *Samain* was one of four annual Celtic festivals. The others were *Imbolc* (February 1st), at which the coming of spring was celebrated, *Beltaine* (May 1st), which revolved around rites to purify cattle, and *Lughnasa* (August 1st), a harvest festival. When Christianity came to the British Isles, these ancient festivals were incorporated into Christian holy days where possible. *Imbolc*, for example, originally devoted to the pagan goddess Brigit, is now celebrated as St. Brigid's Day. *Samain* has become All Saints' Day.

Activity

Your group may want to share their knowledge of holidays from their own cultures as well as associated cultural beliefs. They can ask parents and other family members to give them suggestions for research ideas that they can pursue and then share with others in the group.

Reading Other Tales

Background Information

There are many variations of folk tales about *selchies*. In one of these, which is closely related to the tale upon which this chapter's play is based, the king of the *selchies* creates a storm that brings the four most successful fishers on one of the islands, Uist, to the Cave of the Seals, where he confronts them in the form of a man with a large scar on his face and one missing hand. When the fishers ask him how he lost his hand he says, "In the battle of survival." He explains who he is and makes them swear on their hunting knives that they will never hurt another seal.

In other tales, *selchies* reward kind fishers who do not hunt seals. In one of these, a female selchie saves three children who are about to drown in a rising tide (they have been playing too close to the water's edge). She rescues them because their father once persuaded another fisher not to kill some of her babies. In yet another tale, a seal gets caught in a net, which he destroys in his attempt to get free. He feels guilty for having damaged the means by which the fisher makes his living. In repayment, he helps the fisher find his way back to land during a storm when he is about to be lost at sea.

Activity

Your group might enjoy reading longer, more detailed versions of one of these tales. They could also make one of these tales the basis for a play script of their own. Two books they can consult for longer versions of the tales summarized here and other tales are:

Cutt, Margaret Nancy. *The Hogboon of Hell, and Other Strange Orkney Tales*. London: A. Deutsch, 1979.

Swire, Otta F. *The Outer Hebrides and Their Legends*. Edinburgh and London: Oliver & Boyd, 1966.

Researching Seals

Information Master 1 provides your group with some information about seals. The individuals in your group could choose to research one of the seals mentioned in the article or another seal species of their choice. Your group can use **Research Master 1** as a guide to gather information. They can then present the information to others along with pictures, using whatever visual aids you may have at your disposal.

Discussing Wildlife Issues

Your group could look through newspapers and magazines to find articles about local, national, or international incidents that have affected wildlife and the world's oceans and lakes. You could then organize a debate around some issues. Possible topics include:

- Should animals be kept in zoos or aquariums?
- Should animals be used in medical research?
- Is it ever acceptable to kill an animal?
- Who should decide how much fish should be taken from the oceans—the government or people who earn a living fishing?
- Which fishing methods should/should not be allowed for fishing? Who should decide which methods can be used?
- What can we do to protect wildlife?

Celtic
Illuminated
Letter

Seals

Most mammals have adapted to life either on land or in the sea. For example, a chimpanzee is a mammal that lives on land, and a whale is a mammal that lives in the sea. Seals need both land and sea to survive. They find their food in the sea, but they give birth to their young on land.

Some kinds of seals use their foreflippers when swimming. They are quite mobile on land because their foreflippers are strong enough to support the weight of their bodies. The Northern Fur Seal, California Sea Lion, and Stellar Sea Lion have these features. Other seals—such as the Crabeater Seal, Leopard Seal, Harp Seal, and Harbour Seal—use their hindflippers for swimming. Their foreflippers are weaker, so they look as if they are crawling when they are on land.

In the waters off the Hebridean islands, there are two kinds of seals—the Great Atlantic Seals, which live in deep sea waters, and the Loch Seals, which are much smaller and stay close to land.

Most seals eat fish and other small creatures they find in the sea. The Leopard Seal mainly eats other seals, especially seal pups. It also eats penguins. Crabeater Seals mainly eat a very small animal called krill, which they find in Antarctic water.

Seals have existed for over twenty-five million years. By the middle of the nineteenth century, several species had nearly disappeared because they had been hunted for their fur and their blubber. Today the greatest threats to seals are pollution in the ocean and large commercial fishing nets. The seals are attracted to the nets by trapped fish, but they can become tangled in the nets and drown.

Seal Research

Choose one type of seal to research and jot information about your seal under the following headings. Use your information to write a report about your seal.

Name of seal: _____

1. What does your seal look like? What colour is it? How big is it?	2. What does your seal eat?
3. In which areas of the world is your seal found?	4. What enemies or problems does your seal face?
5. Describe your seal's habitat.	6. List any other interesting facts you discovered about your seal.

The Gharial and the Monkey

About the Play

This play is based on a popular Hindu folk story from India. A gharial sees some monkeys playing in the trees and decides that she'd like to eat fresh monkey heart. Her husband tricks a monkey into going for a ride on his back so he can drown her. When the monkey realizes she has been tricked, she in turn tricks the gharial into returning her safely to dry land. "The Gharial and the Monkey" is part of a folk tale tradition in which a little hero outwits a much larger, usually tyrannical enemy.

Gharials are the sole surviving species of gavials, a member of the crocodile family. Gavials differ from other crocodiles in the slenderness of their snouts. A male gharial can grow as long as seven metres and has a roundish outgrowth on the end of its long snout. A female gharial can grow up to five metres in length. Gharials spend much of their time in the water, but come out to bask in the sun for a few hours each day.

Monkeys are respected in Hindu culture and can often be seen wandering through temple grounds unhindered. According to Hindu mythology, the monkey king, Hanuman, helped rescue Rama's wife, Sita, when she was kidnapped by a demon named Ravana. This incident is celebrated during an annual Hindu festival called *Diwali*.

"Namasté" is a greeting used in the play that is often heard in India. It is pronounced "namastay."

India is a country with a large and varied population. There are many languages and cultures to be explored, including the Hindu culture. For further information on the many cultures of India, consult the following books:

Beck, Brenda E.F. et al. *Folktales of India*. Chicago: University of Chicago Press, 1987.

Bothwell, Jean. *The First Book of India*. New York and London: Franklin Watts, 1978.

Field, Dorothy. *In the Street of the Temple Cloth Printers*. Vancouver, B.C.: Pacific Educational Press, 1996.

Kalman, Bobbie. *India: The Land*. Toronto and New York: Crabtree, 1990.

———. *India: The Culture*. Toronto and New York: Crabtree, 1990.

Madryga, Roxanne and Osborne, David. *A Sourcebook of India: A Multicultural Perspective*. Vancouver, B.C.: Pacific Educational Press, 1986.

Suggestions for Performing the Play

General information on play performance can be found on pages 5-7. "The Gharial and the Monkey" has 4 speaking parts. Other students can play important non-speaking parts portraying the river, as well as other monkeys, gharials, or trees if desired. The play takes approximately 10 minutes to perform.

An important aspect of the play is the tree that Kapi and Bala climb up to elude the gharials. A two-tier set would give the monkeys something to climb onto to represent their clambering up the tree. Stage steps or blocks would work well, but are not necessary. The art crew could use green crepe paper or something similar to dress up a chair or a desk/chair combination as the tree. This tree can also be the same tree that Kapi and Mrs. Gharial drink their tea beside. It should be set up on one side of the stage, close to the audience, so Mrs. Gharial and Kapi do not "see" what is happening during the river scene. During this scene, they should freeze so that they do not distract the audience from the main action.

The river should be onstage throughout, and will probably take up most of the stage or playing area. See the suggestions for scenery for ways to represent the river and Bala and Mr. Gharial's trip across it. Your group can have some fun improvising different ways to represent the sailing trip, especially Mr. Gharial's slithering type movement.

If there is someone in your group who knows traditional Indian dances, you might encourage them to teach others in the group how to perform one. The presentation of a dance before the play starts is a good way of involving more children in the performance while establishing the play's cultural setting.

Suggestions for Scenery, Props, Costumes, and Music

Scenery

India is a very large country and encompasses many kinds of terrain. Your group will need to decide whether it would like the play's setting to be in the mountains or in low-lying land near the ocean and then conduct research to find out about the trees and other plants in the selected area. To represent the forest, your art crew could:

● paint a backdrop mural to show an Indian forest
● use large decorated cardboard cutouts for trees that would be found in an Indian forest
● decorate themselves or other children as trees
● project suitable slides onto a wall or curtain

There are a number of ways in which your performers can represent the river. Here are two. Pairs of students could hold long strips of green or blue material between them and kneeling or crouching low, would gently manipulate the material to make it ripple back and forth to look like a river flowing. Bala and Mr. Gharial move through the river—that is, between the strips. They would need to walk back and forth between the strips as they complete their journey. The "river" performers could dress in the same colour as their strips of material if they will be seen by the audience.

Alternatively, your actors could portray individual waves, making costumes out of green crepe paper and/or cardboard. The "waves" could move across the stage or playing area either in rows or in a horseshoe shape around Bala and Mr. Gharial, bobbing up and down.

Bala and Mr. Gharial would appear to be moving, although they are really standing still.

Props

Your group will need to organize several props for its performance of "The Gharial and the Monkey." Lots of mangoes are needed. These mangoes can be made in a variety of ways—with coloured crepe paper and diluted glue, or with cardboard and paint, for example. The river island's mangoes should be larger and more colourful than the mangoes Bala and Kapi are eating at the beginning of the play.

Your group could have some fun putting together Mr. Gharial's copy of *The Gharial Times*. It could have large headlines that reflect some "crocodile" issues—from the gharial's point of view, of course! Mr. Gharial will also need a container that he can wear on a string around his neck to carry his cargo of a single mango. This, like the mango, can be made of crepe paper or cardboard, which could be cut into leaf shapes. A pair of leaves could be glued together around the edges, with an opening left for the mango.

Your group will also need tea cups for Mrs. Gharial's tea party. If your group wants to make these, they could decorate the cups with Indian motifs.

You will need one last thing—a "nut" for Mr. Gharial to toss in his game of heads and tails. Your group might find it amusing to put a monkey head on one side (depending on the nut's size, they could use a monkey mask for this) and a gharial tail on the other.

Costumes

General instructions for decorating and assembling masks and breastplates can be found on page 7. Specific instructions for decorating and assembling this play's masks and breastplates are provided here.

Gharial Costumes

To decorate the gharial masks and breastplates, use white tissue paper, tempera paint, Rhoplex® or a light water-based glue, and paint brushes. Paint stripes of different shades of green, brown, and purple on a sheet of white tissue paper. When the tissue paper is dry, tear it into small pieces and glue the pieces onto the costumes pieces. When they have been completely covered with tissue paper, brush them lightly with Rhoplex® or glue. This will cause the colours to bleed into each other and will also strengthen the costumes.

The gharial mask pattern includes a snout and a nose bulge, but the bulge is for the male gharial only. Cut along the heavy black lines on the main part of the mask to make the eyes, mouth, and nostrils, and to give the eye area a three-dimensional effect. Be careful not to cut line "C" all the way to the eye sockets. Attach the nose bulge to the male gharial snout *before* attaching the snout to the mask. Cut out the bulge and fold it along the fold line. Fold and glue tabs F and G to the other side of the bulge, following the direction arrows on the master. Cut along the thick black lines through both halves of the bulge and then plump the bulge. Insert tabs E and D of the bulge through slots E and D on the snout, and then tape the tabs in place. Next fold the snout along the two fold lines before attaching it to the mask. Glue the tips of the snout marked A and B to A and B on the mask. Fold and slip the tab on the snout marked C through slot C on the mask and tape the tab to the back of the mask.

Monkey Costumes

To decorate the monkey masks and breastplates, use pencil or wax crayons in browns, black, greys, gold, yellows, purples, and white. Layer colours like brown, yellow, gold, and white on top of each other to create an interesting mottled fur effect. Try to achieve a light and dark effect by varying the pressure applied to the crayon. One monkey will need bright yellow ears, to match the description given by Mrs. Gharial in the play.

Cut the heavy lines around the monkey's ears so they will pop out, and fold along the fold lines on the neckline area to create a ruffled effect. Also cut out the eyes, nostrils, and mouth. Cut the black lines above the eye area to help give the mask a three-dimensional effect.

The monkey mask has furry eyebrows to decorate and attach. Fold tabs A and B on the eyebrows and glue the backs of the tabs to glue spaces A and B on the mask.

For the monkey breastplate, attach the ruffle by putting glue along its A edge and pressing the ruffle along the A glue spaces on the breastplate.

Music

There are many possibilities for musical accompaniment to this play. One choice could be a piece of classical Indian music, possibly featuring the sitar, an instrument used in both classical and folk music from India. Ravi Shankar is a well-known classical musician and recordings of his performances and compositions are widely available. Or your group could select some Indian folk music or a piece of contemporary Indian music such as *bhangra*, which is based on folk music traditions. Environmental music featuring forest sounds may also be considered.

The Gharial and the Monkey

Scene 1. *Mr. Gharial is reading* The Gharial Times.

Mrs. Gharial *(urgently)*: Mr. Gharial! Darling? Come quick! I want you to see these monkeys!

Kapi and Bala enter eating mangoes. Mr. and Mrs. Gharial watch them from behind a tree.

Kapi: I have never—*ever!*—tasted such sweet mangoes.

Bala: Here's to our most successful fruit gathering day ever!

Kapi: I just wish it wasn't such hard work. It seems like we spend half our day swinging through trees looking for fruit that we eat in less than two minutes!

Bala: Yes, but mangoes this sweet make it worthwhile.

Mrs. Gharial: Just look at them! They look so plump and juicy.

Mr. Gharial: The mangoes?

Mrs. Gharial: The monkeys! I particularly like the looks of the one with the bright yellow ears. It has been such a long time since I've had a really tasty monkey heart for dinner. Why don't you ever catch a monkey for me anymore? You used to catch them all the time when we were first married ...

Mr. Gharial: Mrs. Gharial! I'm not as young as I used to be! Catching monkeys is hard work. They're tricky little things!

Bala: Kapi! Gharial alert!

Mrs. Gharial: Oh! He's seen us!

Kapi: Quick! Up the tree!

Mr. Gharial *(to Mrs. Gharial)*: Don't worry! I'll handle this. *(He makes himself look as tall and brave as possible.)* Namasté, monkeys.

Kapi: Namasté, gharials.

Mr. Gharial: We couldn't help but overhear you. If you think those mangoes are sweet, you should try the mangoes on the island in the middle of the river. They are the sweetest in the world.

Kapi: Are they really? I've never heard that before. Have you heard about the mangoes on the island, Bala?

Bala: No, and we've lived in this area for ages.

Mr. Gharial: Well, it's true. The island's mangoes are world famous.

Mrs. Gharial: You haven't told them the best part, Mr. Gharial.

Kapi: Oh? What's that?

Mrs. Gharial: The mangoes are so large and so ripe they fall off the trees and drop to the ground. Talk about easy pickings!

Kapi and Bala look at one another in excitement.

Kapi: What a nice change of pace that would be, just to pick our dinner off the ground.

Mrs. Gharial: I see you swinging from tree to tree all day long and I feel sorry for you. You really should treat yourselves to some of the island's mangoes.

Mr. Gharial: I just happen to be travelling over to the island today.

Kapi: *Really?*

That's wonderful! Can you bring us back some mangoes?

Mr. Gharial: I'd love to. But I can only carry one at a time.

Mrs. Gharial: And that one's for me!

Kapi: That's too bad. You've really whetted my appetite.

Bala: Mine, too! I really must taste one of those famous mangoes.

Mrs. Gharial: I always say that with a little ingenuity you can solve any problem.

Bala: There must be *some* way ...

Mr. Gharial: What I suggest is that one of you, whoever is braver ...

Kapi and Bala stand up tall and strike heroic poses:

Mr. Gharial: ... ride over to the island on my back. Then you can bring back as many mangoes as you like.

Bala and Kapi do not look quite as brave as they did a moment ago.

Kapi: It's such a tempting offer ...

Bala: But we would need certain guarantees.

Mrs. Gharial: Of course! Such as?

Kapi: Whoever goes over would want to go and come right back, without any delays.

Mr. Gharial: That's no problem. I don't have any other business on the island.

Mrs. Gharial: And he has to be back in time for dinner. So which one of you would like to be the brave adventurer?

Kapi and Bala together *(pointing at one another)*: She would!/He would!

Kapi: I wouldn't dream of putting my interests before yours, Bala. *You* should go.

Bala: Oh, *no.* You work so much harder than I do! You deserve this holiday. I insist that *you* go.

Mrs. Gharial: I'm sure you'll both get a chance to go eventually ... But who's going to be the lucky monkey today?

Mr. Gharial: The mature thing to do—the adult thing to do—is to toss a nut.

Mrs. Gharial: I have one right here!

Bala *(to the audience)*: What a coincidence!

Mrs. Gharial: Heads or tails?

Kapi *(gulping)*: Heads.

Mrs. Gharial: All right, here we go!

Kapi puts his hands over his eyes and Bala puts her hands over her ears. Mrs. Gharial tosses the nut.

Mrs. Gharial: Well, what do you know, it's tails! That makes you the lucky winner, Bala!

Bala and Kapi look at one another.

Bala *(to the audience)*: Isn't that wonderful?

Kapi: Could I speak to you alone for a moment, Bala?

Bala: Certainly.

Kapi draws Bala aside.

Kapi: Are you sure you want to go through with this?

Bala: This could be the easiest mango haul of our lives! If it's successful, we could sit in the shade of a tree and eat mangoes for days without lifting our fingers.

Kapi: *If* it's successful. I've never met a gharial I could trust. They're always thinking of their stomachs ... if you know what I mean.

Bala: Kapi! I'm surprised at you! A gharial is no match for a monkey. Trust me.

Mr. Gharial: Let's get going, Bala.

Kapi: Have a safe trip, Bala!

Mrs. Gharial: Don't you worry about Bala! She'll have a wonderful trip. Let me pour you a cup of tea.

Mrs. Gharial pours a cup of tea and makes Kapi sit down under the tree with it.

Mr. Gharial *(to Bala):* Climb onto my back, Bala.

Bala: See you soon, Kapi.

Mr. Gharial: We'll be back before you know it.

Scene 2. *Bala and Mr. Gharial set "sail" across the river.*

Mr. Gharial: If you don't mind, Bala, we had better not talk. I have to give my full attention to navigating.

Bala: By all means! Keep your eyes on the water! I'll do the talking.

Mr. Gharial: Please, Bala, I'd prefer it if we could sail in complete silence.

Bala: Mr. Gharial, complete silence is impossible for a monkey. You know what chatterers we are. Eat and talk, eat and talk, that's all we do. Until we get to the island I can't eat. Talk is all I can do.

Mr. Gharial *(to the audience)*: If I let her talk I'll never be able to go through with it. It's now or never.

Mr. Gharial makes a ducking movement.

Bala: Mr. Gharial! Was that a wave? I thought only the ocean had waves.

Mr. Gharial: It was no wave.

Mr. Gharial makes another ducking movement.

Bala: Mr. Gharial! What are you doing? Monkeys can't swim! If I fall into the river, I'll drown. You *promised* me a safe journey.

Mr. Gharial: And I promised my wife a monkey's heart.

Bala: A monkey's heart? What for?

Mr. Gharial: What *for*? To eat, of course.

Bala *(laughing)*: Why didn't you say so? You don't have to drown me to get my heart. In fact, if you drown me, you'll *never* get it.

Mr. Gharial: What do you mean?

Bala: A monkey's heart is a precious thing! You don't think I brought it with me, do you?

Mr. Gharial: Well, of course you did. You don't have any choice. You mammals need your heart to function. It pumps blood through your veins and keeps you warm and alive.

Bala: Most mammals need their hearts all the time, but not us monkeys. Our hearts are detachable. I only wear mine on special occasions, like birthdays and festivals.

Mr. Gharial (*laughing*): You don't expect me to believe that, do you? I'm not a fool! I'm an *educated* gharial.

Bala: Would I lie to you, Mr. Gharial? Listen, as your friend, I'm prepared to make a special sacrifice on your behalf. After we get the mangoes and return to land, I'll run home and get my heart, and you can give it to your wife.

Mr. Gharial: Oh, no. We'll get the heart first, then we'll go to the island for mangoes.

Bala: That seems so silly when we're almost there. You'll have wasted a lot of energy for nothing. You're too old for that, Mr. Gharial. You've got to think of your own heart.

Mr. Gharial: You're a true friend! All right. We'll get the mangoes first. But as soon as we get back to the mainland, you must run straight home and get your heart.

Bala: It's a deal.

Bala and Mr. Gharial "sail" off-stage.

Scene 3. *Mrs. Gharial's tea party beneath the trees.*

Kapi (*nervously*): They've been gone an awfully long time.

Mrs. Gharial: Oh, I'm sure they'll be back any time now.

Mrs. Gharial curls up to sleep under one of the trees. Bala and Mr. Gharial "sail" onto the stage again. Mr. Gharial has one mango in his leaf-shaped container. Bala holds several mangoes in her arms.

Kapi: Bala!

Bala: Kapi! Can you help me carry these mangoes home? Mrs. Gharial has asked Mr. Gharial to get her my heart. And Mr. Gharial has been *so* helpful that I have agreed to run home and get it to give to him.

Mr. Gharial (*nodding*): Yes, Bala, please go get it right away. I'm going to wake up my wife, and let her know how pleasantly this has turned out!

Bala: You do that! We'll be back soon. (*to Kapi*) Let's get out of here!

Kapi: Are you kidding? There's no way I'm missing the look on Mrs. Gharial's face when she hears how badly her little plot turned out. Quick! Up this tree!

Mrs. Gharial wakens.

Mrs. Gharial: What took you so long? I was beginning to think that something had gone wrong.

Mr. Gharial: Just the opposite, my dear. Everything has gone very, very well.

Mrs. Gharial: Well, where's the heart? Let me have it. I want to marinate it in some snail juice.

Mr. Gharial: I don't have it just yet, but it should be here any minute.

Mrs. Gharial: What do you mean?

Mr. Gharial: Bala has just run home to get it.

Mrs. Gharial: Run home to *get* it? What on earth are you talking about? Do you think that a monkey's heart is *detachable*?

Mr. Gharial: Well, yes. That's what Bala said.

Mrs. Gharial: Mr. Gharial! You've let that monkey outwit you.

Mr. Gharial: Oh, no! That can't be true!

Kapi and Bala wave from the trees.

Kapi: Namasté, Mr. Gharial!

Bala: Namasté, Mrs. Gharial!

Kapi: You can't ever catch us, Gharials, because you can't climb trees!

Mr. Gharial: Bala! You promised to give me your heart! Where is it?

Bala *(thumps her chest)*: My heart is right here, safe and sound, and right here is where it's going to stay.

Mrs. Gharial *(to Bala)*: You just wait! You may have outwitted my husband but the day will come when you won't be able to outwit me.

Kapi *(holding up a mango):* Long live clever monkeys!

Bala: I'll eat to that!

Gharial Mask

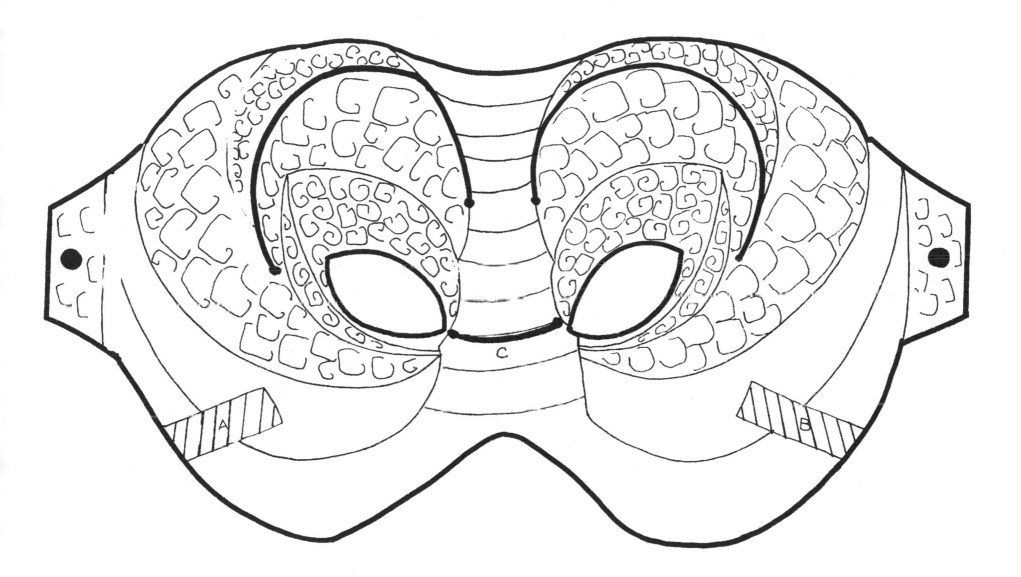

**Gharial Snout &
Nose Bulge**

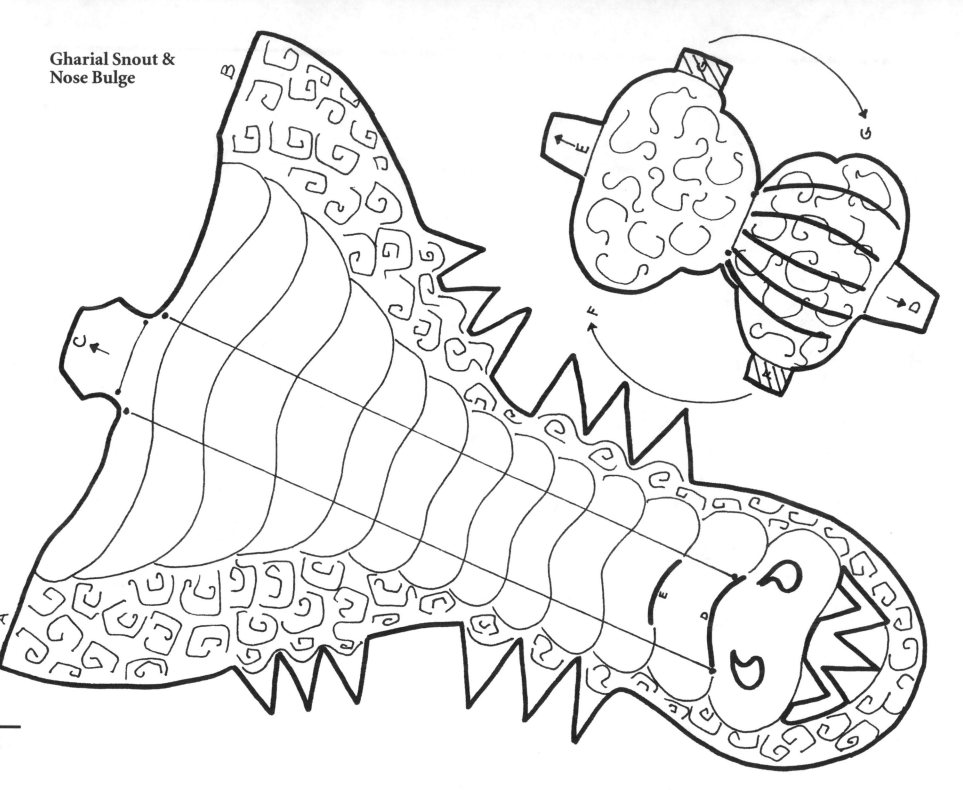

Gharial Breastplate

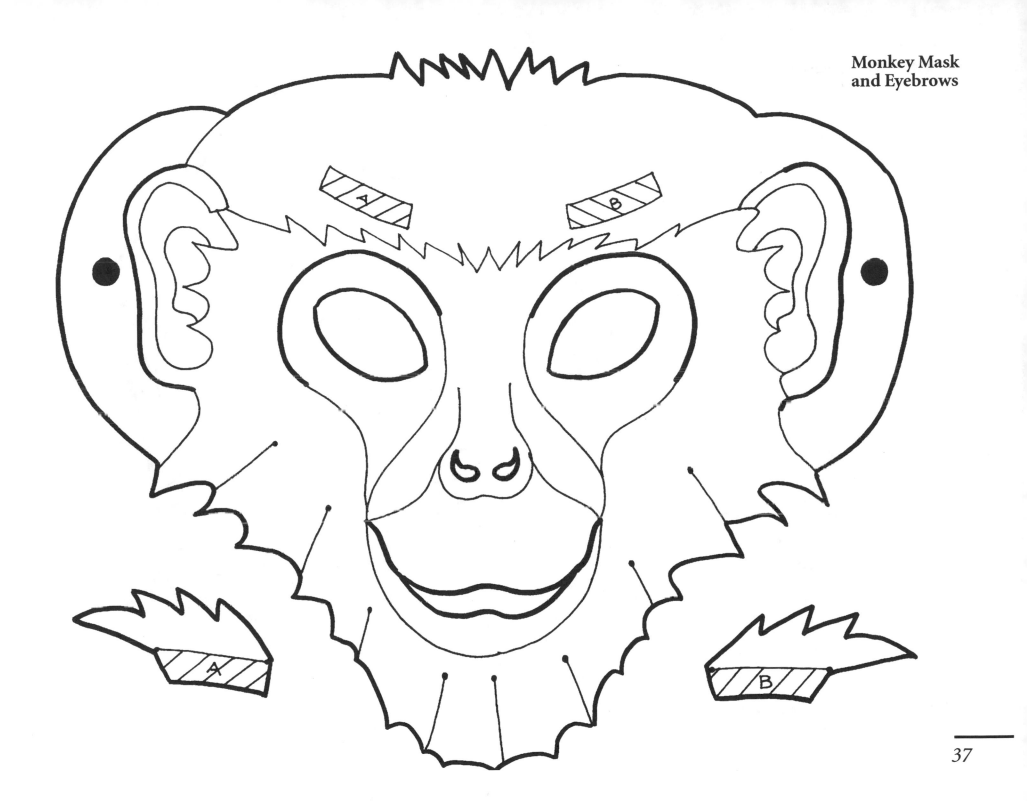

**Monkey Mask
and Eyebrows**

Monkey Breastplate

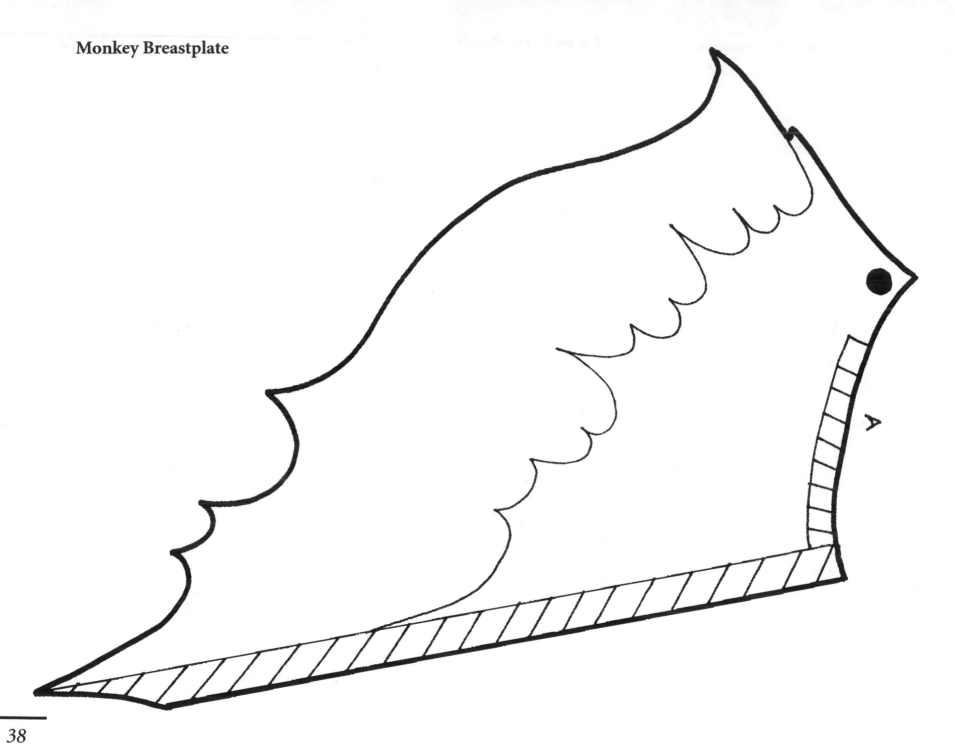

A

A

A

Activities

Researching Mother Ganges
Background Information

High in the Himalayas, flowing from the Gangotri glacier as it melts, is the source of India's most sacred river, the Ganges. Indians call the river *Ganga Ma,* Mother Ganges, and her source in the Himalayas they call *Gaumukh,* the mouth of the world.

For at least 2,500 years, the goddess Ganga has been revered. Hindus believe that the Ganges River *is* the goddess. Her entire length is studded with *tirthas,* holy places at which the goddess can be venerated. At *tirthas,* Hindus cleanse themselves of all their sins by drinking and bathing in the goddess Ganga's waters. The first of the *tirthas* is at a pool of icy cold waters in the Himalayas called *Gauri Kund. Saddhus,* wandering holy men, come from all over to India to bathe in *Gauri Kund* and meditate at its side. At the other *tirthas* along the Ganges' 2000 kilometres, there are *ghats,* steps which descend into the river to make it easy for worshippers to bathe. The most famous of these bathing places are at Prayag, Hardwar, Nasik, and Ujjain—the four mythical resting places of the god who stole some of the Ganga's nectar. Every twelve years, when Jupiter, the earth, the sun, and the moon come into line, special bathing festivals called *kumbh melas* are held. Millions of Hindus journey to one of these four sites to take part in the mystical purifying process. Hindus believe that nothing can cleanse them of their sins as certainly and completely as the waters of the Ganges, and that if they are cremated near the Ganges or have their ashes scattered on its waters, they will have a place in heaven assured for them. Professional water carriers take the sweet waters of the Ganges to all parts of India. Nothing can affect the sweetness of these waters, it is believed, and nothing can make them go bad. It is even believed that the Ganges has the power to kill cholera and dysentery germs.

Activity

Your group may want to find out more about the Ganges. They could research crocodiles and gavials, which are found in the Ganges river delta; the *susu* or Ganges dolphin, a black mammal with a long thin snout that picks small fish out of the river's muddy bottom; or snow leopards that make their home along the river's bank. They could find out about various threats to the purity of the Ganges, like the sewage plants that have made the waters at Varanasi, India's holiest city, undrinkable and unsafe to bathe in. They could research Hindu bathing festivals and funeral ceremonies. Or they could find and share myths about the Ganges and the goddess Ganga. Two useful books for children to use for research are:

Arya, Aditya and Jagmohan Mahajan. *The Eternal Ganga.* New Delhi: Spantech Publishers, 1989.

Saith, Sanjeev and Mukul Kesavan. *A Journey Down the Ganga.* New Delhi: Lustre Press, 1989.

Retelling Indian Folk Tales
Background Information

Animals play a role in Indian life that goes beyond the various parts they play in India's environment. As part of the Hindu philosophy of *ahisma,* respect for all living things, certain animals are venerated. The most famous of these worshipped animals is the cow. Cows are never eaten by Hindus and are revered as "mothers" of India because they give milk.

The elephant is another animal that plays a special role in Indian life. The Koruba tribe of Southern Mysore, for example, use elephants to help them harvest trees. Elephants may be among the earth's largest creatures but they are also very gentle. Young men in the Koruba tribe train elephants to pick their way carefully through forests to pull down individual trees without harming others in the immediate vicinity. The youth who trains an elephant is called a *mahout;* a *mahout* and his elephant often develop a special bond. Both cows and elephants are celebrated in special festivals throughout India for which the animals are decorated with paint, flowers, and bells and are led in procession.

The special relationship between Indians and animals is also revealed in the incarnations of Hindu gods. Sometimes the god is part animal—Ganesh, for example, has an elephant head. Sometimes the incarnation is entirely animal—Vishnu, for example, is often shown in the form of a boar.

Activity

To help children gain a further understanding of the cultural importance of animals in India, they may want to read folk tales in which animals play a part. In order for the children to be exposed to as many tales as possible, each child could find and read a different tale. Encourage the children to read their tales until they can retell them in their own words. Then hold a storyteller's time, where the children can share their tales with each other.

Finding Out about Tea

Background Information

Tea was first introduced to Europe at the end of the fifteenth century by Portuguese explorers. The famous Dutch East India Company was the first to establish an east-west trade in tea. During the early part of the seventeenth century, tea was a luxury that only the very wealthy could afford, but by the end of the century, it was being sold by apothecaries for medicinal purposes.

Tea is an important crop for India for both economic and cultural reasons. There are Chinese and Japanese legends that claim that India was the original home of the tea plant, where it grew wild. But it was not until the late eighteenth century that cultivation of tea was attempted in India under British rule.

Activity

Information Master 2 provides some background information about tea. Your group could use it as a starting point to research the process of manufacturing tea (picking, withering, fermenting, etc.); a type of tea (green tea, black tea, herbal tea, etc.); the role of tea in their culture or family; or where tea is grown in the world. Or they may like to find out about the various beliefs surrounding the medicinal uses of tea; the

history of the explorations that led to the "tea trade;" or the cultivation of tea in India by the British. Children could share the results of their research through maps, charts, written reports, or any other presentation form they like.

Researching Origins of English Words

Background Information

India is famous for the beautiful fabrics and fabric patterns it produces. Its silks were first introduced to the western world at Rome around 50 B.C.E. Nothing like this light, iridescent fabric had ever been seen there before and silk was considered as valuable as gold. It is believed that silk originated in China. Legend has it that silkworm eggs and mulberry seeds (silkworms eat mulberry leaves) were spirited into India from China by a Chinese princess who was being married to an Indian prince and who wished to bring her beloved silks with her. It is India, not China, however, that made the production of silk into an art and a huge commercial enterprise. India's silks have been exported to Europe since at least the twelfth century, along with its muslins. Muslin is an Indian invention. It is a cotton fabric so fine that you can see through it. Its fineness has earned it many poetic names, one of which is "woven winds."

In India, silk is used to make various articles of clothing like saris, turbans, and bandanas. The Indian textile industry has been so important to the world that many Indian textile words have found their way into other languages like English—words like muslin, bandana, jodhpurs, and pajamas (in Hindi, *pa* is the word for leg and *jama* is the word for garment). Paisley, now a common English word, was a pattern invented in India which became fashionable in England in the nineteenth century and was thus adopted as an English word. Taffeta is another example of a textile word that has an Indian origin.

Activity

Using the words provided here as a starting point, your group might like to research words from other languages that have found their way into English. Children could work in pairs to choose a language to research. After identifying some words, they could write short definitions or histories of the words. All the words could then be put together in a dictionary of "Words from Other Languages."

Designing a Central Panel for a *Kantha*
Background Information

In Bengal, the *kantha* is a quilt that is a unique and beautiful example of folk art. Bengali quilts were traditionally made from yellow wild silk. The silk was embroidered with Indian motifs but later, when Indian silk became a popular export to countries in Europe, the designs on them incorporated European motifs as well.

In the centre of a *kantha,* there is usually a lotus flower, the symbol of Lakshmi, goddess of bounty and prime deity of Bengal, and a frequently-used motif in Indian art. Around the flower, Bengali quilt-makers stitch common artifacts of their lives, religious symbols, and animals (particularly the elephant and the horse).

Activity

Your group can create their own central design for a *kantha.* They can begin by drawing a flower in the middle of a piece of paper, and surrounding it with drawings of important things in their lives. The flower on a Bengali quilt is usually simple and stylized, a circle with elongated petals attached, and the symbols are often duplicated to form patterns around the flower. Since this is paper, not fabric, your group will need to colour rather than stitch the flowers and symbols. They can use bright golds, oranges, reds, and greens to duplicate the colours often found in these quilts.

Tea

Tea is an ancient beverage. It is believed that the aboriginal peoples of Burma and Thailand were the first to drink tea, thousands of years ago. They plucked the leaves from trees on which it grew wild. Tea was first cultivated in China, however, where the Chinese used it as a medicinal herb. The word "tea" comes from the Chinese character for tea, which is pronounced "tay" in Cantonese. From China, the cultivation of tea spread to Japan, and according to one story it was the Buddhist monks who took tea with them when they travelled from China to Japan. Today tea is grown in many parts of southeast Asia, and it is widely consumed around the world.

Wild tea is a small evergreen tree that grows about five to ten feet high. Tea needs well-drained soil, good rainfall, and a tropical or sub-tropical climate to thrive.

Tea grown for commercial use is planted on large plantations. Tea trees are pruned into bushes about three feet tall. Pruning produces more buds. The bud and its two youngest leaves make the highest quality tea. For regular tea, the bud and several leaves from each small twig are picked.

After the tea leaves are picked, they are dried and shredded. To make black tea, the kind most often found in Canada, the tea leaves are then fermented. Oolong tea is partly fermented.

The tea is then graded. The best grade is orange pekoe, followed by pekoe, souchong, congou, and pekoe dust. Darjeeling tea, which grows in India in the foothills of the Himalaya Mountains, is regarded as one of the world's finest quality teas.

Tea is one of India's most important crops. The most important tea-growing areas are in the northern states of Assam and Bengal. Tea is both a "cash crop," a crop sold to other countries, and a crop grown for the use of the Indian people. The amount of tea grown in India has doubled since 1950. Tea is sold at large tea auctions in the Indian cities of Calcutta and Bombay and in London, England. Thousands of buyers and brokers congregate at these auctions. Brokers play a key role in the tea industry; they taste all the tea to be sold at auctions in order to determine how much it should be sold for.

Tea is enjoyed in many different ways by people around the world. In Britain, people drink it with milk and sugar, or with lemon. The British invented a new meal around tea: "high tea." Iced tea is popular in the summer in North America. The people of Nepal often add yak milk butter to their tea. In India, people add spices like cardamon, ginger, cinnamon, and pepper to green tea. Black tea is drunk without milk but often with a pinch of salt to prevent the drinker from getting dehydrated in very hot weather. In Japan, green tea is preferred, and the Japanese have developed a special tea ceremony.

The Great Frog

About the Play

"The Great Frog" is based on an Australian folk tale. It takes place in the Dreamtime of long ago before the coming of humans. It tells of a frog who swallows all the water on earth. The other animals try to make the frog laugh so he will release the water, but are unsuccessful until a little eel comes to the rescue.

It is easy to understand why this particular myth was so important to Australia's Aborigines whose migrations around their continent were always constrained by their need to stay close to a source of fresh water. In the deserts of central Australia, water is so important that Aborigines would measure distances between places in terms of how many watering places lay between one place and another. Each aboriginal tribe had a terrain that it regarded as its "country," which was always centred around a watering place. Each tribe believes that its ancestors originally settled around their watering place and that the spirits of the ancestors wait at their watering place for reincarnation in future generations of the families of the tribe. In periods of severe droughts, desert frogs drink as much water as they can before burying themselves in the earth where they wait for the rains to return. As a last resort during these times of drought, when there was not a drop of water available at the watering place, Aborigines would unearth these frogs and drink the water inside them.

Some books that may contribute to your understanding of the Australian aboriginal culture include:

Kwork, Kwork the Green Frog and Other Tales from the Spirit Time. Canberra: Australian National University Press, 1977.

Eugene, Toni. *Strange Animals of Australia: Koalas and Kangaroos.* Washington: National Geographic Society, 1981.

Hoyt, Olga. *Aborigines of Australia.* New York: Lothrop, Lee & Shepard, 1969.

Lawrie, Margaret. *Myths and Legends of the Torres Strait.* New York: Taplinger Publishing Company, 1970.

Morgan, Sally. *The Flying Emu and Other Australian Stories.* New York: Alfred A. Knopf, 1993.

Mountford, Charles. *Before Time Began.* Melbourne: Nelson, 1976.

Oogeroo. *Dreamtime Aboriginal Stories.* New York: Lothrop, Lee and Shepard Books, 1994.

Robinson, Roland. *Aboriginal Myths and Legends: Age-Old Stories of the Australian Tribes.* London: Paul Hamlyn, 1969.

Suggestions for Performing the Play

General information on play performance can be found on pages 5-7. "The Great Frog" takes approximately 8 minutes to perform, but may be extended by having Koala tell her story aloud to the Great Frog so the audience can hear it too. This story could be made up or a retelling of another aboriginal folk tale. The play has 8 speaking parts. Several non-speaking actors are needed for the Great Frog's body. To include more members of your group in the performance, you can incorporate more trees into the play and have another eel.

A suggestion for how to represent the water coming out of the Great Frog's mouth—as a shower of paper waterdrops—is included in the stage directions for the play. Your group could brainstorm and choose another way if they wish. One way is to have performers with long blue scarves run from the Great Frog.

Eel's dance should be exuberant and funny in order to make the Great Frog laugh. You may wish to have all members of your group contribute ideas for the dance to help the actor.

The narrator can be on- or off-stage.

Suggestions for Scenery, Props, Costumes, and Music

Scenery

Australia is a country of many terrains and climates. The play is set somewhere that experiences monsoonal rains after months of hot, dry weather, such as the open eucalyptus forests of northern Australia. To create an Australian scene for this play, your group could research the flora of this region. The actors playing trees could be costumed to look like one of Australia's many acacia trees or one of its over 600 species of eucalyptus trees. You may want to paint other trees onto a backdrop along with some of Australia's shrubs and grasses such as saltbushes, bottle brushes, fringe flowers, and porcupine grasses.

To show what the play setting would like like during times of drought, your art crew could paint a backdrop depicting an Australian desert scene. The crew could research some of the unusual rock formations and plants found in the Australian deserts, and they could use the same desert colours suggested for the costumes.

Props

Among the props you will need are a dry leaf for Koala to crush and another so she can fan herself. These can be made out of crepe paper and cardboard respectively. An imitation lily leaf like one of the giant lilies that are found in Australia's billabongs would be ideal for the fan.

Another important prop is the water-carrying object in which Lizard pretends his foot is trapped. The aboriginal peoples of Australia carried water in various ways—in tightly woven grass baskets, in kangaroo skins, in folded palm leaves, and in bark bailers. Of these, the easiest to make is an imitation bark bailer. For this you could use cardboard that is painted brown. You might want to decorate the bark bailer with a water symbol from Australian aboriginal art. A grasshopper might be a good choice since it is associated with the lightning that precedes monsoonal rains. You could look for aboriginal representations of grasshoppers in books on aboriginal rock art. You could also use symbols from aboriginal rock art to create symbol-covered papier mâché rocks for your set. Consult this chapter's activities for further information on aboriginal symbolism.

Costumes

To decorate and assemble the masks and breastplates, follow the general instructions on page 7. For this play, follow these specific instructions.

To colour the costumes, the children could use coloured felt pens, pencil crayons, tempera or poster paint, paint brushes, and flat-ended sticks. Your group might like to use Australian desert colours like browns, oranges, yellows, greens, greys, black, light blues, light purples, and white. Suggest that the group discuss the colours they wish to use for the different animals so the costumes are not too similar. The designs on the masks and breastplates include symbols used in aboriginal art.

Lizard Costumes

Remember to paint both sides of both pieces of the lizard frill. To make the lizard frill, fold along the fold lines, folding one line over the other in the direction of the arrows. Fold the tabs under, and glue the A tabs to the A glue spaces on the mask, and the B tabs to the B glue spaces. Make sure that the two halves of the frill cover the entire glue spaces on the mask—from the centre of the forehead to the lizard's chin.

Koala Costumes

For the koala ears, fold along both fold lines on each of the ears before inserting the ears into the A and B slots on the koala mask. Remember to cut out the lines above and below the nose on the koala mask to make the nose stand out.

Eel Costumes

For the eel mask, make sure to cut the heavy lines inside the mask, including those in the centre of the forehead. Fold the glue tab on the fins before attaching to the mask.

Wombat Costume
Insert the ears into the appropriate slots on the mask and tape. Glue the whiskers onto the mask.

Great Frog Costume
For the frog eyebrows, fold along the fold line for the A tab. After cutting the dark line in the middle of each eyebrow, glue or tape the shaded area to the area behind the dark line to make a dart. After inserting tab A into slot A, the eyebrows need to be secured by putting a little glue behind the shaded areas on the ends of the brows. Then press the shaded areas onto the corresponding shaded areas beneath the frog's eyes.

Music
The music chosen for the eel's dance should be lively. Possible choices for other music include environmental music of the desert or traditional Australian aboriginal music.

The Great Frog

The Great Frog is sitting in the middle of the stage looking full and very contented with himself. The actor who will speak for the Great Frog sits on top of a high stool. Five or six other actors cluster around the stool as the Great Frog's body. They hold the rolls of blue ribbon and the bucketfuls of blue and green paper water drops that represent the earth's water.

Narrator: This story is from the aboriginal people of Australia. It tells of the Dreamtime long ago when the world began, and spirits had the form of animals, birds, and fish. During the Dreamtime, there lived an enormous frog. He was so large that when he hopped, the earth rumbled, and when his shadow fell on the land, day became like night. One day the Great Frog awoke feeling very thirsty. First he drank the lakes until all the lakes were dry; then he drank the rivers, creeks, and billabongs, until all the rivers, creeks, and billabongs were dry. Soon there was not a drop of water to be found anywhere in Australia.

Two gum trees droop and drop their leaves.

Tree 1: It's so hot!

Tree 2: We need water! What are we going to do without water?

Koala enters.

Koala: I am *so* thirsty! I have looked everywhere, and there's not a drop of water to be found anywhere. What am I going to do? I can't live without water. *(She kneels down in front of the Great Frog.)* Please, Great Frog, won't you let me have some water?

The Great Frog does not respond. Koala sits down under one of the drooping trees. She pants with thirst, crumbles a dry leaf in her hand, and looks miserable. The frilled Lizard enters.

Lizard: Whew! It's so hot and dry. Where has all the water gone? I can go for days without water, but I can't go without it forever. I'm getting worried.

Koala *(pointing to the Great Frog)*: *He* drank it all. It's stored in his stomach and he won't give it back. *(The Great Frog rubs his stomach.)*

Lizard: He drank all of it? That's impossible! Do you know how much water there is in the world?

Koala: I know how much there is, but believe me, he drank it all. I've begged him to give me some, but he doesn't seem to care whether anyone else lives or dies.

Lizard: Perhaps we have to reason with him. If I give

him all the facts, he's bound to change his mind and let us have some water. That's what any reasonable frog would do.

Lizard moves over to the Great Frog and bows before him.

Lizard: O Great Frog, I humbly request that you hear our petition. I am sure Your Greatness had good reasons for drinking all of the earth's water, every drop of it. But I'm afraid we must ask you to give some of it back. We need water to live! If you don't share the water with us, we'll all die and you'll be left all alone, the only creature on the planet.

The Great Frog continues to stare straight ahead.

Koala: See, he just ignores us. It's so unfair! It's so cruel of him! If I don't have a drop of water soon—just one little drop—I think I'll die.

Lizard: Don't die yet! Reason may not work, but I'm sure something else will.

Wombat enters.

Koala: Here comes wise old Wombat. Maybe she'll know what to do.

Wombat: Oh where, oh where, has all the water gone?

Lizard: We've found the culprit. It's the Great Frog. He's drunk every last drop.

Koala: And he won't listen to a word we say. He ignores our petitions. He won't show any mercy. He's the cruellest, most selfish frog in the whole world!

Lizard: And the largest.

Koala: How can you make jokes at a time like this?

Lizard: It keeps our spirits up!

Wombat: But it doesn't get us any water. We have to find a way to convince the Great Frog to share the water. I'll talk to him.

Lizard: I've already tried reasoning with him. He'll just ignore you.

Wombat: Yes, I suppose you're right. I've heard that he's not a very reasonable fellow. Then we'll have to think of something else.

Koala *(wailing)*: What can we do?

Wombat: I've got an idea. Koala, I've heard that you tell very funny stories. Isn't it true that you kept a circle of your friends laughing all through the night once with your stories?

Koala *(woeful)*: Yes, it's true.

Wombat: Why don't you tell the Great Frog one of your funny stories, the funniest one you can think of? If he laughs, water will pour out of his mouth and back into the rivers and the lakes.

Koala (*wiping a tear from her eye*): I'm not feeling very funny at the moment. But I can try.

Koala walks over to the Great Frog and curtsies before him.

Koala: O Great Frog, I have come to offer you my services as an entertainer. May I tell you a story?

The Great Frog nods. Koala goes and whispers in the Great Frog's ear.

Koala: Isn't that funny? Isn't that a scream?

Koala laughs so hard she falls to the ground and rolls around laughing. After a minute she looks up to see if the Great Frog is laughing as well. The Great Frog is staring ahead, just as he has been from the very beginning.

Koala (*wailing again*): It didn't work. He didn't even smile!

Lizard: Maybe your story just wasn't funny enough.

Wombat (*patting Koala on the shoulder*): Or maybe it was very funny, and the Great Frog just didn't get it. Perhaps we should try some physical comedy. You're good at that kind of thing, aren't you, Lizard?

Lizard (*swaggering*): I've made a few people laugh in my time.

Wombat: Well, come on! Let's see something *really* funny.

Lizard: All right.

Lizard bows before the Great Frog.

Lizard: Great Frog, you are about to witness the funniest sight you have ever seen.

Lizard crosses to Koala and whispers in her ear. Koala doesn't look very convinced, but she crouches down obligingly. Lizard takes a few steps back, then runs at her, and leaps over her. Everyone except the Great Frog laughs.

Lizard: Isn't that the funniest thing you ever saw? A lizard leaping over a koala? I'll bet you thought only frogs could leap over things. (*Aside to everyone except the Great Frog*) Not that he could leap over anything right now with that belly full of water!

Koala: He's not impressed.

Wombat: It looks like you're not any funnier than Koala, Lizard. Not as far as the Great Frog is concerned.

Lizard: What a failure! All I did was make myself thirstier.

Wombat, Koala, and Lizard all look desolate. Then Lizard brightens.

Lizard: I have another idea.

Lizard holds up a finger and runs off into the wings. He returns immediately with a bailer. He saunters over to the Great Frog swinging the bailer and whistling. When he reaches the Great Frog he puts down the bailer.

Lizard *(in a loud voice)*: I know you *say* you've drunk every drop of water in the world, Great Frog, but I'm sure there must be a watering hole *somewhere* that you've missed. I am going on a mission! If you won't give us some water, we will find some for ourselves!

Lizard deliberately steps backwards into the bailer. He holds the bailer with his foot in it in the air and jumps around on his other leg.

Lizard: Oh, no! I can't get my foot out! Help! Help!

Lizard hops over to Wombat and Koala still pretending to struggle to get his foot out of the bailer.

Lizard: Is he laughing?

Koala: No!

Lizard sets down the bailer in disgust, and looks dejected.

Lizard: Well, I don't know what it's going to take. That's the funniest gag I know.

Lizard, Wombat, and Koala sit in a circle and huddle together miserably. Koala fans herself with a large lily leaf.

Koala: I can't take any more of this heat unless I have some water!

Eel enters.

Eel: Well, hello there! Perhaps you can tell me what's going on. There's no water *anywhere*. I can't find a place to swim.

Wombat *(wearily)*: The Great Frog—*him*, over there!—has swallowed all the water, every last drop, and he won't give it back. He doesn't care whether we live or die. We've been trying to make him laugh so that his mouth will open and water will pour out.

Eel: You've been trying to make him laugh? Well, that's easy. *I* can make him laugh.

Koala: You can? How?

Lizard: You're just a little eel. What can you possibly do to make him laugh?

Eel: Ha, ha! Watch me now and you will see!
I can dance though I've no feet.
Just give me the music and give me the beat.

Music begins to play.

Eel: Hello, Great Frog! I've come to dance for you!

Eel starts to dance slowly and then begins to contort his body wildly. The Great Frog looks up and takes notice.

Great Frog: Ha! Ha! Ha! *(The children who form the Great Frog's body roll out the water ribbons and toss their blue paper waterdrops.)* What a funny little eel! You're the funniest little eel I've ever seen! And I've seen a lot of eels in my time.

Wombat, Koala, Lizard and Eel rush over to the water. Wombat and Koala scoop up handfuls of the paper waterdrops and shower them over their heads. Lizard and Eel each pick up a water ribbon and wind it around their bodies.

Koala: Water! Water!

Wombat: Oh, what a relief!

Lizard: How refreshing!

Eel: I've never enjoyed a swim so much.

Tree 2: Water, sweet water!

Tree 1: We can drink and grow strong again.

The trees bend to the water then stretch their arms as high as they can.

Koala: You're such a clever little eel.

Wombat: I'm proud of you, little eel.

Lizard: Well done, little eel. The whole world thanks you!

Frilled Lizard Mask

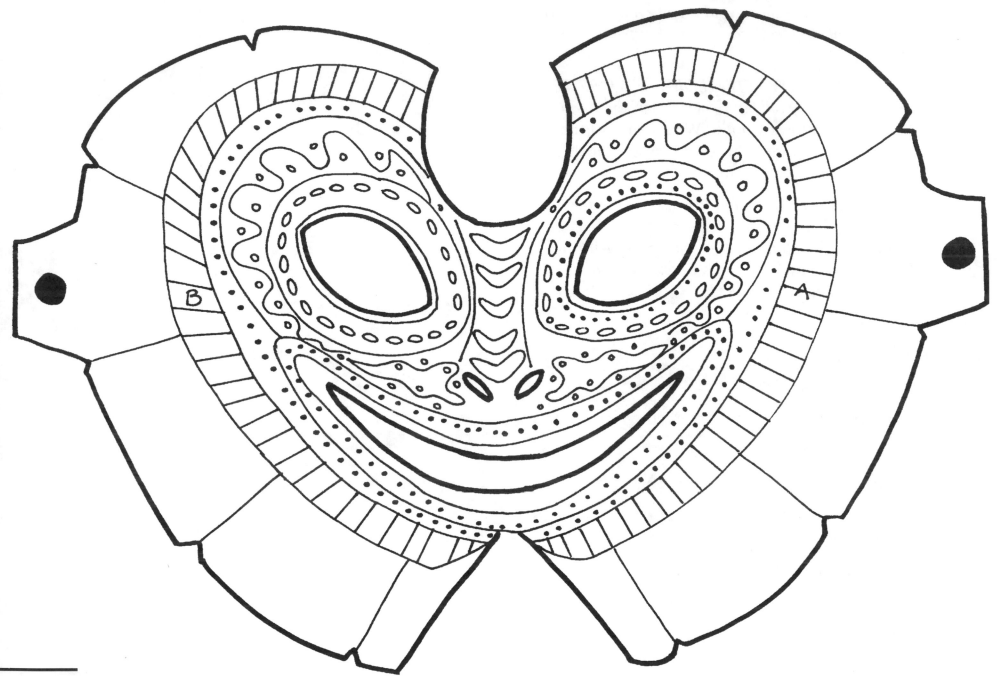

Lizard Frill

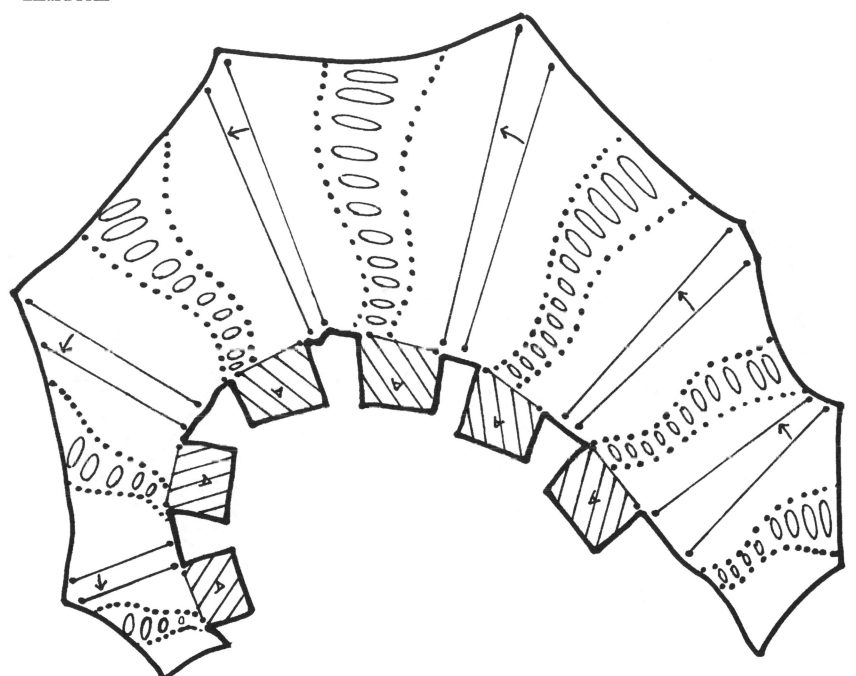

Lizard Frill

Frilled Lizard Breastplate

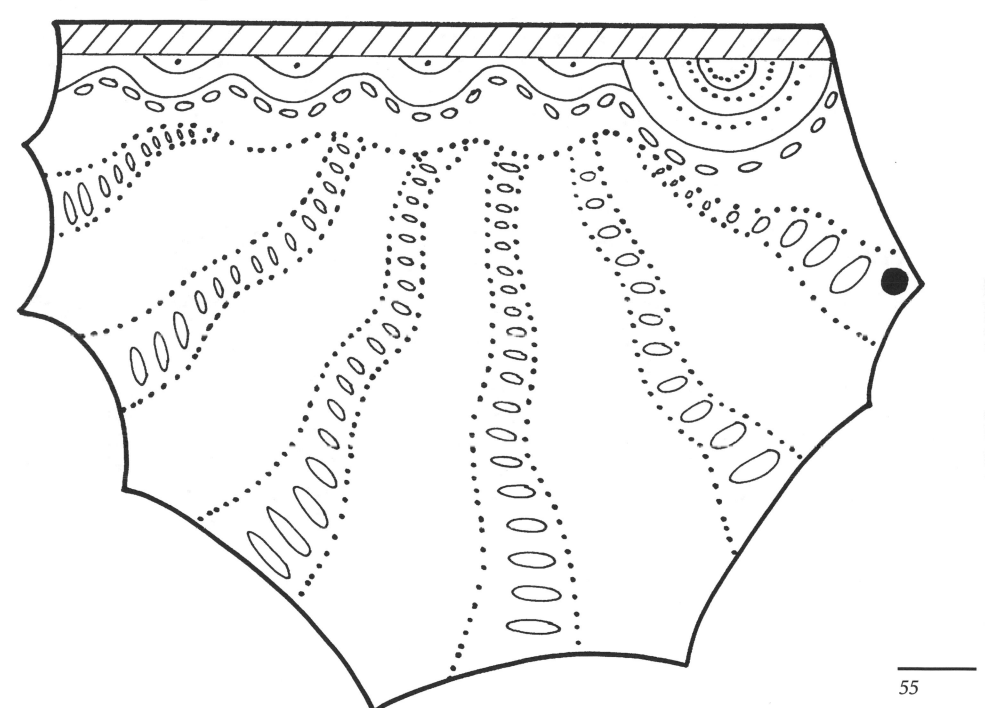

Frilled Lizard Breastplate

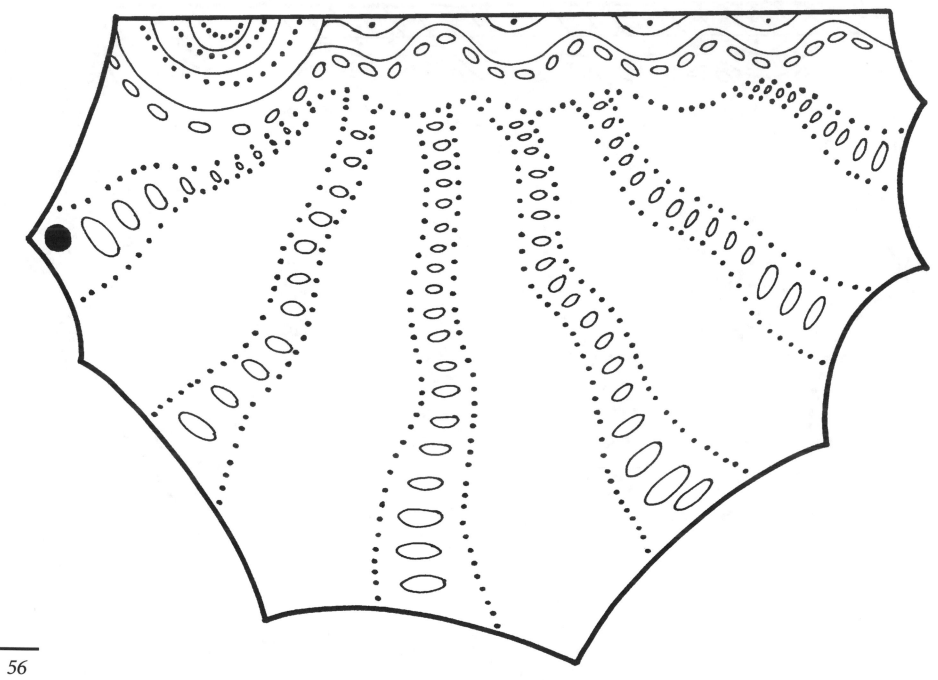

Koala Mask

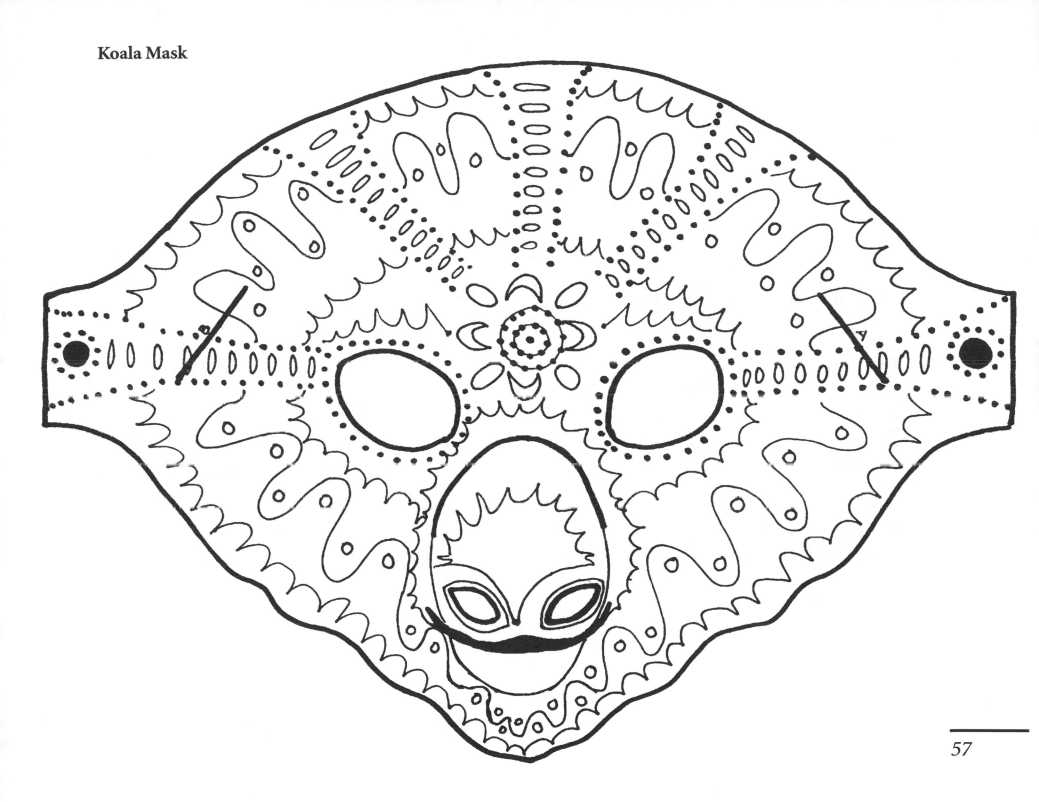

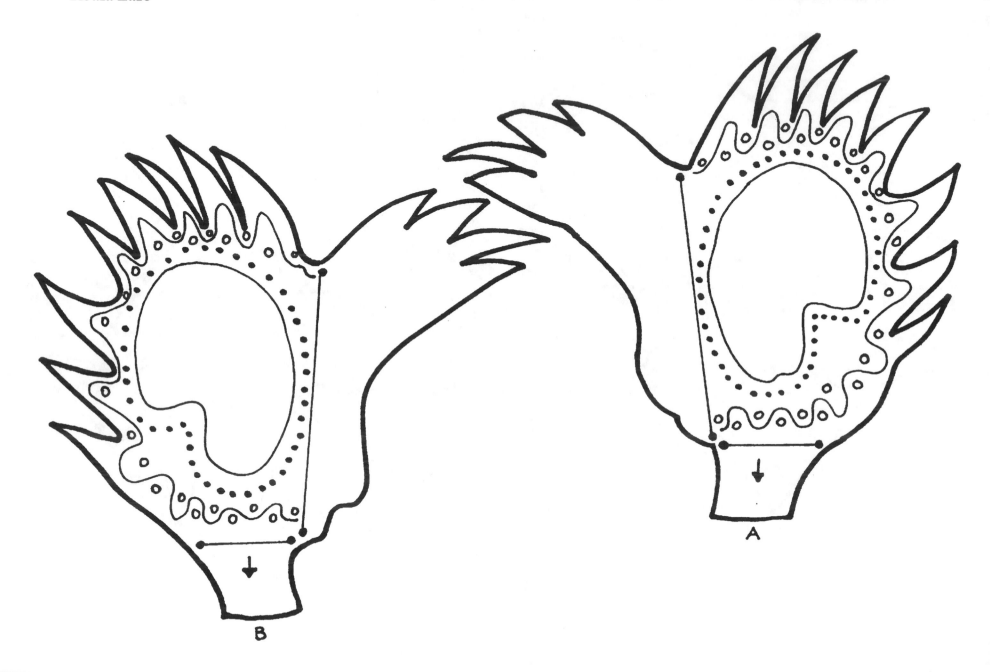

Koala Breastplate

Koala Breastplate

Eel Mask

Eel Breastplate and Fin

Eel Breastplate and Fin

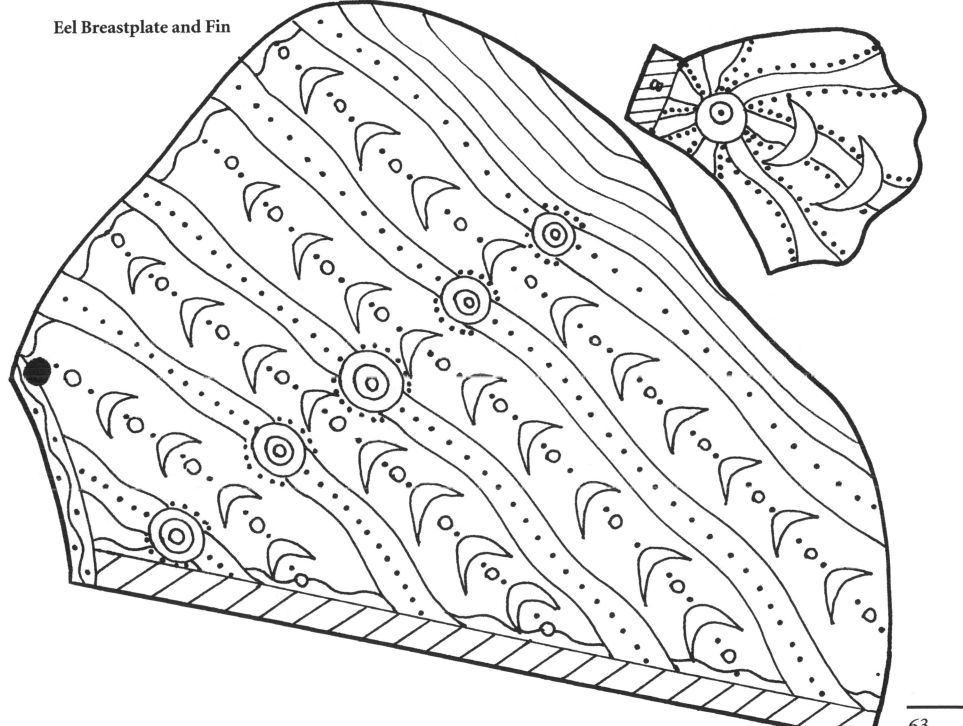

63

**Wombat Mask, Whiskers,
and Ears**

Wombat Breastplate

Wombat Breastplate

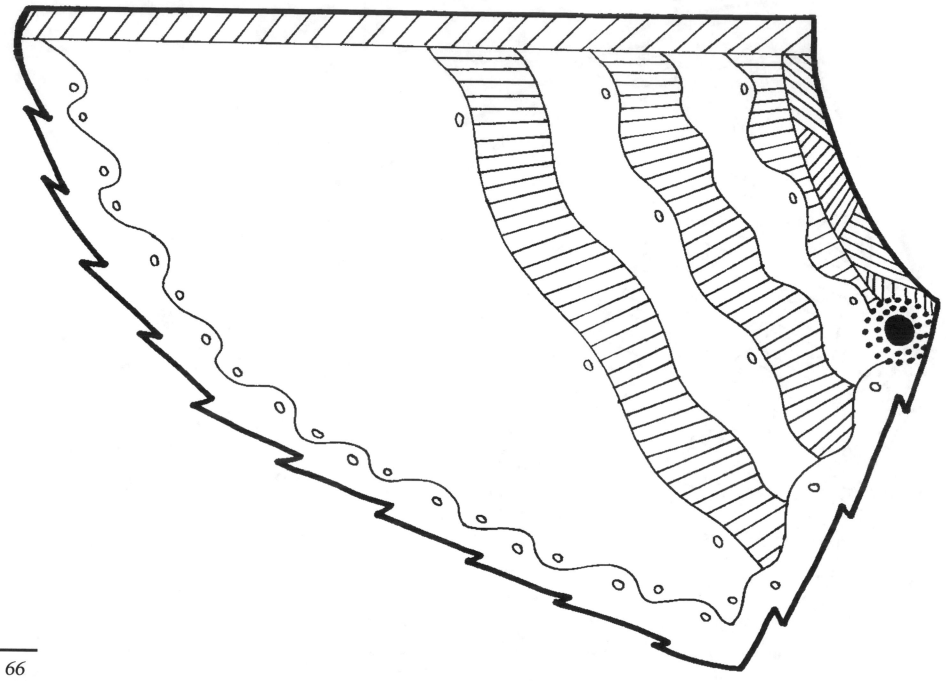

Great Frog Mask

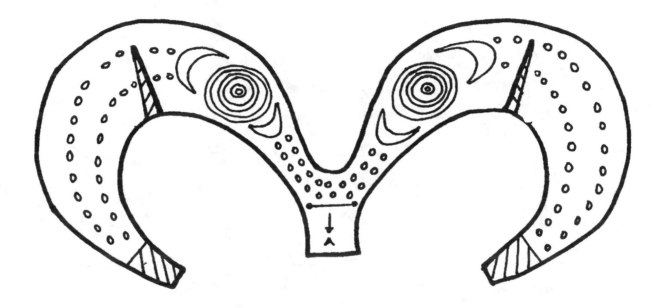

Great Frog Breastplate

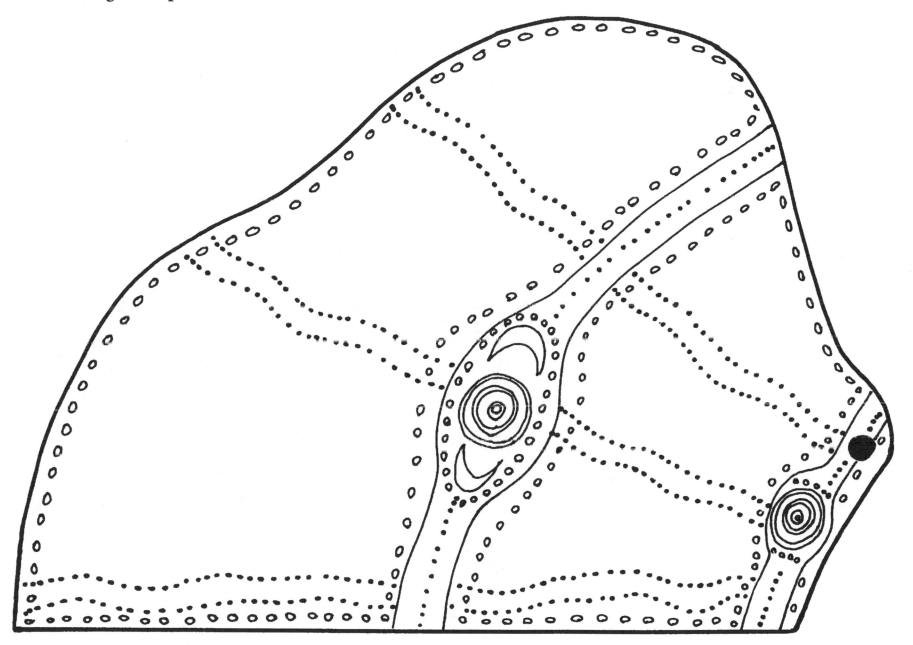

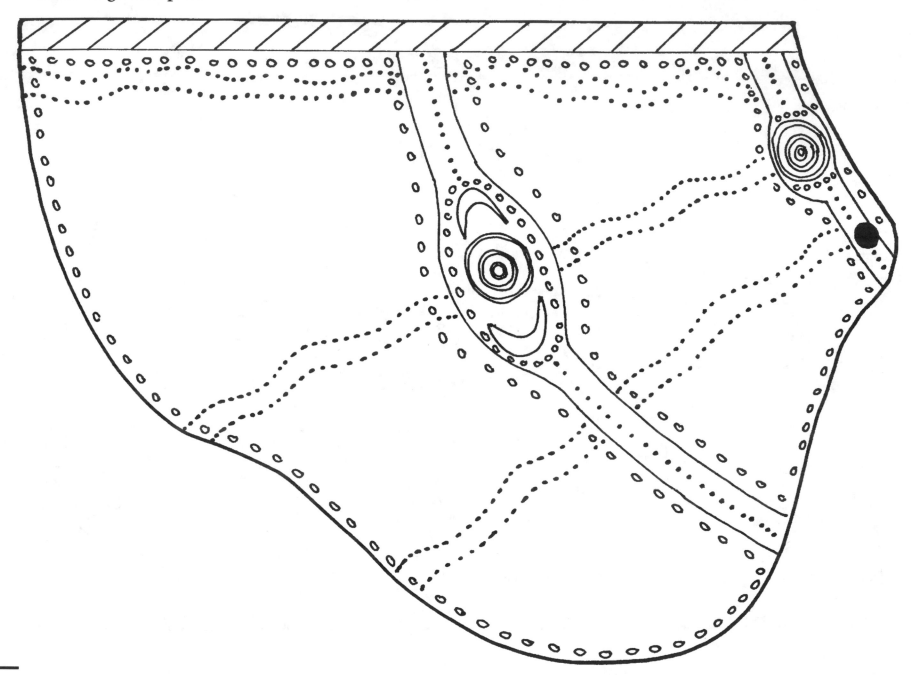

Activities

Researching Australia's Archaeological Sites
Background Information

Australia is in many senses a living museum. Its unique geographical history—created by its migration away from the other continents when Pangaea, the original land mass, split—means that there are forms of life flourishing on the Australian continent that can no longer be found elsewhere on the planet. The stromatolite, for example, one of the single-celled organisms from which it is believed the rest of life on earth may have evolved, can still be found at places like Shark Bay in western Australia. The Christmas Bush—a red and green bush that flowers at Christmas time—is unique to Australia, as is the kangaroo. Australia is also a paleontological treasure house. At Lake Mungo in New South Wales (southeastern Australia), the skeleton of Mungo III—a man buried over 30,000 years ago—has been found. Elsewhere in Australia paleontologists have discovered bones of gargantuan creatures dating from the same period. The aboriginal peoples called these massive creatures *Kadimarkara*, and have myths about other creatures like the *bunyip* and the *yowie* which they believe existed in Dreamtime, the period in which their giant ancestral spirits strode across the continent following their "dreaming tracks" and creating the landscape and everything in it as they travelled. The Aborigines themselves may be among the planet's oldest surviving groups of humans.

Many aboriginal myths, such as the one that the centre of Australia was once a lush paradise and that Kangaroo Island was separated from mainland Australia by a new post-Ice Age Sea, are supported by current scientific theories. Aboriginal myths have been kept alive mostly by oral storytelling, but the aboriginal peoples have kept their myths alive in another important way—through their rock art. Through stencilling, engraving, and painting with ochre pigments, Australia's aboriginal peoples have celebrated their belief in Dreamtime and recorded key symbols of their beliefs for tens of thousands of years. In 1989, archaeologist Rhys Jones discovered stone tools and ochre paintings that date to at least 40,000 years ago. Uluru (formerly called Ayer's Rock), the red monolith which is perhaps Australia's most famous prehistoric rock formation, is engraved and decorated with many aboriginal symbols. The Aborigines believe that Uluru is one of the many features of the Australian landscape created during Dreamtime. By decorating landmarks like Uluru as well as their bodies with symbols of their Dreamtime ancestors, Aborigines believe they keep these ancestral spirits happy and gain access to the creative and spiritual power that the ancestors represent.

Activity

Your group may wish to break into smaller groups to research Australia's important archaeological sites such as Uluru, or to learn more about Mungo III and other discoveries of prehistoric remains, or to find out about other sites sacred to the Aborigines. The results of this research could be presented in a number of ways. Some groups might like to hold "mock" interviews with archaeologists about their discoveries, or with Mungo III about life in Australia 30,000 years ago. Or they could "guide" others through a tour of a site by using photographs and maps.

Experimenting with Symbols and Stencilling
Background Information

Many symbols used in aboriginal art are of animals. Australia's Aborigines have traditionally had great respect for animals. Each group within an aboriginal tribe has a particular species of animal that it regards as its totem. The group will not hurt or eat an animal of this species unless its survival depends on it. Even then, the group will only kill an animal from its totem species after an elaborate ceremony. A particular group's symbols will often embody the stories of how their animals came to be their totems. Sometimes the symbols are of vegetables like yams that a tribe depends upon for sustenance. Symbols of a group's totem were often used in rock art. More complex figures found in ancient rock art include men with boomerangs; Namarrgon the Lightning Man; men dancing; the crocodile; the Rainbow Serpent; and various representations of the Wandjina and other Dreamtime ancestors.

Stencilling is another ancient aboriginal art form. The stencilling of hands is one of the most popular images in the caves and the rock shelters that are sacred sites for Australia's Aborigines.

Activity

Have your group read **Art Master 2** to find out more about symbols used by aboriginal artists. It would also be interesting for them to see some aboriginal art in art books. The children could then experiment with symbols and stencilling in a number of ways. They could:

- make stencils of their hands and use them to decorate objects
- use the symbols from the Art Master and others they make up to tell a story in the aboriginal fashion
- create their own art pieces using their own symbols.

Finding Out about Camouflage

Background Information

The Great Barrier Reef, the world's most famous series of coral reefs, extends 2,000 km (1,250 miles) from Torres Strait at the tip of Cape York Peninsula along Australia's eastern coast to southern Queensland. Coral reefs are built by tiny marine plants and animals called polyps. These polyps build their own limestone shells or stone houses to protect themselves from predators. During the day the polyps remain within their stone houses, but at night they extend their long, phosphorescent tentacles to try to catch even smaller marine plants and animals to eat.

The reef provides fascinating examples of camouflage. It provides protection to other forms of sea life, especially small fish, who make their homes among the coral from which they are largely indistinguishable. One kind of fish that can camouflage itself among the polyps of coral reefs is the damsel fish.

Activity

Your group could read **Information Master 3** to find out more about how animals use camouflage to protect themselves. Then they could choose an animal that uses camouflage to research, using **Research Master 2** to organize their work. After the research is completed, they could work together to make a book about these animals, including pictures and/or drawings along with information in paragraph or point form. Two books for children that provide information about animals found in the Great Barrier Reef are:

McGovern, Ann. *Down Under Down Under: Diving Adventures on the Great Barrier Reef.* New York: Macmillan, 1989.

Sargent, William. *Night Reef: Dusk to Dawn on a Coral Reef.* New York: F. Watts, 1991.

Reading Origin Myths

Background Information

Almost every culture has its own myths that explain how the earth and all things on it were created. These origin myths, as they are known, sometimes explain how the first day occurred; how the first woman and man came to live on earth; how the sun and the moon ended up in the sky; why the earth experiences phenomena like earthquakes; and how animals acquired their distinguishing features. As noted earlier, most of Australia's Aborigines believe that the earth and everything on it were created by Ancestor Spirits who sprang mysteriously out of nothing to create things as they moved; but the Aborigines themselves have alternate versions of this story. One of the most colourful claims is that a rainbow shattered into myriad pieces that fluttered to land in the form of various birds, butterflies, other insects, and animals. This is just one example of an origin myth variant on a single continent. The planet's numerous variations on these myths often represent attempts to adapt the story to fit the particular aspects of a people or a region. The Naga peoples of India, for example, believe that a spirit called Lijaba created the world. Lijaba was, for the most part, a very careful worker who took great pride in the work of creation. But while Lijaba was working on Nagaland, a giant cockroach interrupted him to warn that certain of his enemies had learned of his whereabouts and would soon reach Nagaland to attack him. Lijaba finished Nagaland in a great hurry; and as a result the region is one of rough-hewn, dangerous mountains and cliffs.

Activity

Your group might enjoy reading and comparing origin myths from different cultures. They could choose a common theme such as how the earth was created, how fire and light came to be, or one of the themes listed in the background information for this activity. Each child could choose a culture, find a myth about the theme, and then share it with the rest of the group. Or they might like to choose a culture, read a number of origin myths from that culture, and share their favourite with the group. Encourage them to discuss the similarities and differences among the myths.

Many of the books suggested for reading elsewhere in *Windows on the World* contain origin myths. Others children could read include:

Courlander, Harold and Wolf Leslau. *The Fire on the Mountain and Other Ethiopian Stories.* New York: Holt, 1960.

Gillham, Charles E. *Beyond the Clapping Mountains: Eskimo Stories from Alaska.* New York: Macmillan, 1954.

Heady, Eleanor and Tom Feelings. *When the Stones Were Soft: East African Fireside Tales.* New York: Funk and Wagnalls, 1968.

Hulpach, Vladimir. *American Folk Tales and Legends.* London: Hamlyn, 1965.

Leach, Maria. *How the People Sang the Mountains Up.* New York: Viking Press, 1967.

Mayo, Gretchen. *Earthmaker's Tales: North American Indian Stories about Earth Happenings.* New York: Walker and Company, 1989.

Creating a Dictionary

Your group may want to develop a picture dictionary of Australian words. Each child could choose a few words and conduct research to write a dictionary entry. Drawings or pictures could also be added. Each word could be on one page, and the pages put together alphabetically to make the dictionary. The following words could be used as a starting point. Two possible entries are provided as examples for the group.

Koala: Koalas are marsupials; females have pouches where their newborn babies live. Koalas live in eucalyptus forests in Australia. They eat the leaves and flowers of certain eucalyptus trees. They don't move around much. They sleep curled up in the limbs of trees, holding on with their feet.

Wombat: Wombats are marsupials. The babies stay in the mother's pouch for six months. Wombats live in burrows in Australia and Tasmania. They have stocky bodies without tails. Wombats are easily domesticated and make interesting pets.

Tasmanian devil	billabong
frilled lizard	echidna
kookaburra	possum
copperhead	numbat
budgerigar	dingo
platypus	emu
kangaroo	wallaby
cockatoo	marsupial
joey	gum tree
monotreme	outback

Australian Aboriginal Symbolism

The aboriginal people of Australia may be the oldest living race of humans on earth. They lived in Australia undisturbed by people from other parts of the planet until the first Europeans reached Australia in the 1600s. The Aborigines lived simply, in close harmony with their environment. They were hunters and food-gatherers. Their knowledge of their land and nature's cycles was so complete they could survive in the harshest of climates with only the simplest of tools.

Most aboriginal myths are concerned with nature. Australia's Aborigines believe that at the beginning of Dreamtime, giant creatures similar to humans rose out of the earth's flat surface and wandered about Australia creating the earth's features and all its creatures, as well as fire and the first weapons. The features and markings of places such as Uluru are, to the Aborigines, evidence of the existence of the mythical beings of Dreamtime.

Because they had no written language, the Aborigines used drawings in the sand to illustrate or tell their stories about the beings from Dreamtime. By passing these stories down from generation to generation, they also passed down their history, their knowledge of the land, and their customs. The symbols were often drawn quickly in the sand, and then erased as the story moved on and the storyteller required new pictures. The symbols were drawn as if seen from an aerial perspective, and one symbol often had several meanings. Now, aboriginal artists draw their pictures on permanent surfaces—even furniture. But they still mainly use four traditional colours—red, black, yellow, and white—ground from earth pigments. Here are some examples of symbols used by aboriginal artists.

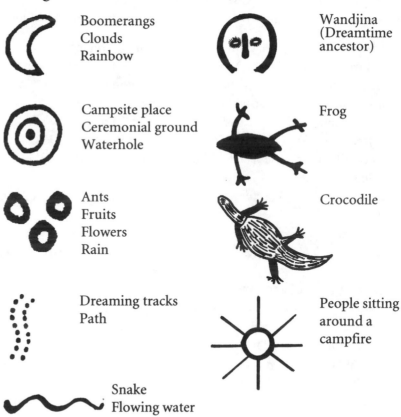

Boomerangs
Clouds
Rainbow

Campsite place
Ceremonial ground
Waterhole

Ants
Fruits
Flowers
Rain

Dreaming tracks
Path

Snake
Flowing water

Wandjina
(Dreamtime
ancestor)

Frog

Crocodile

People sitting
around a
campfire

Camouflage

A creature's colouring or shape often acts as a form of protection, allowing it to blend with its surroundings so that it is not easily seen by its enemies. This is called camouflage. Some animals such as the chameleon can even change their skin colour within a few minutes so that they can blend in with the colours of their surroundings. Rays can also change colour to camouflage themselves in the ocean.

Some butterflies are camouflaged because the undersides of their wings are brown. When they are on the ground and their wings are folded, they look like dried leaves. Stick insects resemble the twigs on bushes and move very slowly so that it's not easy to see them.

A tiger's stripes are uneven in shape and colour, giving the animal an irregular outline so that it may blend readily with the shadows of the forests where it lives. A graded shade of fur, usually darker on top and lighter below, patterned fur, or spots all help camouflage an animal.

Some animals are similar in colour to their surroundings. For example, the tawny colouring of a lion makes it difficult to find when it is in the dry brownish grass of the East African grasslands. Many frogs have the same colouring as their habitat. Tree frogs are often greenish in colour, while frogs that live on the ground are brownish. The leafy sea dragon is a type of sea horse. It lives among the seaweeds of the ocean, and its colouring is very much like seaweed.

Some birds not only use their colouring to camouflage themselves, but also strike poses to hide themselves better. Screech owls have feathers that resemble tree bark. They close their eyes and stretch very thin, and in this way, often pass for a stubby broken branch.

Some animals change colour according to the season so that they are more difficult to see. For example, the snowshoe hare is brown in summer and white in winter.

This leafy sea dragon looks like a piece of green seaweed, which helps protect it from its enemies.

Camouflage Research

Research an animal that uses camouflage and jot information about the animal under the following headings.

Name of animal: _____

1. Describe your animal's habitat.	2. What type of camouflage does it use?
3. How does camouflage help the animal?	4. What does the animal like to eat?
5. Who are the animal's enemies?	6. What other interesting facts did you learn about this animal?

The Tiger's Whisker

About the Play

"The Tiger's Whisker" is based on an Indonesian folk tale. The play is about a little mouse deer who saves her island from the war threats of a neighbouring tiger king by pretending that a porcupine's quill is actually their queen's whisker. This is an example of a trickster tale, a type of tale common to many of the world's cultures.

Indonesia is one of the largest countries in the world, having a population of over 200 million and covering an area of nearly 2,000,000 square kilometres (741,000 square miles). It consists of over thirteen thousand islands. The Indonesian archipelago lies in the Pacific Ocean to the north and northwest of Australia. Indonesia's six largest islands are Sumatra, Java, Bali, Kalimantan, Sulawesi, and Irian Jaya.

Indonesia is a place of many different religions, Hinduism and Islam among them. The Indonesian national motto—"Unity in Diversity"—reflects a centuries-old Indonesian philosophy called *gotong royong*, a belief in the interdependence of people and the need for mutual assistance. We see the principle of *gotong royong* at work in the play when the porcupine does not hesitate to help the beleaguered mouse deer even though he need not fear the tigers to the same degree. The tiger officers and tiger advisers in the play act according to another important Indonesian ideal, *musyawarah untuk mufakat,* when they try to reach all their decisions through a process of conference and consensus-reaching.

A mouse deer is a ruminant (chevrotain) that weighs about 2 kilograms (over 4 lbs). It lives in the tropical forests of southeast Asia.

For more information, the following books will be helpful:

Fyson, Nance Lui. *Indonesia*. Austin, Texas: Steck-Vaughn, 1990.

Mirpuri, Gouri. *Indonesia*. New York: M. Cavendish, 1990.

Smith, Datus Jr. *The Land and People of Indonesia*. New York: J.B. Lippincott, 1983.

Southall, Ivan. *Indonesia Face to Face*. Melbourne: Lansdowne Press, 1965.

Stewart, Ian Charles. *Indonesia: Portraits from an Archipelago*. Singapore: Concept Media, 1983.

Weatherbee, Donald. *Ancient Indonesia and Its Influence in Modern Times*. New York: Franklin Watts, 1974.

Suggestions for Performing the Play

General information on play performance can be found on pages 5-7. "The Tiger's Whisker" takes approximately 10 minutes to perform. The play has 11 speaking parts and 3 non-speaking parts. You can include more members of your group in the performance by having extra, non-speaking tiger officers, tiger advisers, and mouse deer.

The play takes place on two different islands, but the same playing area or stage can represent both islands if the stones that represent the bridge between the two islands are cleverly placed. The stones could be laid close to the audience in a semi-circle that arcs from one side of the stage to the other. The hornbill and the tiger officers will travel across the bridge to return to the same playing area, which, after the trip, will represent the mouse deer island. Encourage all members of your group to take part in deciding how this crossing of the bridge might be presented in a military way. This will make the tiger officers' hurried flight across the same stones at the end of the play even funnier in contrast. The hornbill and the tiger officers should not return to the playing area after their final flight; once they have recrossed the bridge, they should exit off-stage. Use tape to mark the spots where performers should place the stones when the bridge is being constructed. To keep the stones from shifting during the performance, the children will need to step on them carefully and avoid having more than one performer on a stone at one time.

When the hornbills go on their reconnaissance mission, they could move on- and off-stage—in and out of the playing space—to suggest their travel. After their second or third movement off-stage, only one hornbill will return. Encourage the performers who are left on-stage waiting during the mission to be inventive in displaying their patience (or impatience!) during this interlude.

Suggestions for Scenery, Props, Costumes, and Music

Scenery

Your group may want to design the stage or playing area to look like a tropical forest. Some Indonesian trees that your group might want to include are banana trees, bamboo, coconut trees, sandalwood, and various palms including the lontar palm. Large cut-out cardboard trees could be made, or fallen tree branches could be used and decorated with the brightly-coloured butterflies of Indonesia, made here from tissue paper. The world's largest flower, the *Rafflesia Arnoldi*, is found in Indonesia. If you are using a stage, your group could paint a large, simple backdrop showing a row of these flowers. If you are performing "The Tiger's Whisker" in the round, tissue paper *Rafflesia Arnoldi* would make a vivid addition to the tissue-paper butterflies.

Your group could take an entirely different approach to their set decoration by using slide images of Indonesia to show the richness of the country's landscape and architecture. The idea is to create a luminescent panel of images that remains projected on a wall or a curtain at the back of the stage throughout the entire performance. You do not want to have slides changing during the play, however, as this will distract your audience.

Props

Two cardboard "whiskers" are needed as props—one small one for the tiger king to send to the queen of the mouse deer and one very large one for the porcupine's quill. The tiger king will have to hide his whisker prop somewhere on him until the moment when he mimes plucking it from his face.

A number of stones are needed as well for the bridge between the islands. Cut circles from cardboard and paint them beige or grey.

Costumes

To decorate, cut out, and assemble the masks and breastplates, follow the general instructions on page 7. For this play, follow these specific instructions.

Tiger Costumes

To colour the tiger costumes, use oil pastels or wax crayons in yellows, oranges, golds, and warm browns. Use different shades of similar colours to create the stripes and blotches of tiger fur. Colours layered on each other may also help give a textured, fur-like effect. Some areas should be left blank and filled in later with black.

When the masks have been coloured, they should be brushed with a black water-based wash. This technique is similar to the tempera paper batik technique described on **Art Master 3**. It will colour the blank spaces and add further texture to the masks. Excess wash may be removed by lightly sponging or blotting the mask with absorbent paper.

While assembling the tiger masks, make sure to fold along the 3 fold lines of the nose, especially the central line for the ridge of the nose. Cut the dark line near the bottom so the nose will pop up.

To attach the tiger eyebrows, you may want to put a touch of glue on the back of the ends of the brows. That way, you can secure the brows to the top corner of each of the eyes.

Hornbill Costumes

Hornbill costumes can be coloured black, grey, or dark brown to match a hornbill's true colours, with the beak a bright red, green, or yellow.

Prepare the hornbill's beak for assembly by folding it along its centre line. Then place glue on the beak's glue tabs to glue the halves of the beak together. Cut out both pieces of the beak's bulge. Glue the bulge's halves together by gluing the tabs on the back of the first piece and matching that piece carefully to the other half. Attach the bulge to the beak by inserting the D tabs on the bulge into the D slots on the beak. Be careful when cutting the D slots. Do not cut all the way to the edge of the bulge. When you have inserted the D tabs into the D slots, tape down the D tabs. Attach the bulge and the beak to the masks by inserting the A and B tabs on the beak into the A and B slots on the mask. Tape down the A and B tabs. Then insert the C tabs on the bulge into the C slots on the mask. Tape down the C tabs.

Music

Possible choices for musical accompaniment include traditional *gamelan* orchestra music or environmental music of a tropical forest. A *gamelan* orchestra is composed mainly of percussion instruments, such as different types of gongs and drums. *Gamelan* music is used in Bali's famous mask dramas and on other social and religious occasions.

Porcupine Costumes

To decorate the porcupine mask and breastplate, you may want to use the wax resist method using wax crayons explained on page 108 under the turtle costume instructions in "The Hare's Liver." Use yellows, oranges, and browns offset with white. Colour the tips of the quills with a white wax crayon. Some areas should be left uncoloured, and the finished masks washed with dark brown paint.

Glue the porcupine's whiskers on at A. Fold back the glue tabs on the tufts of fur and glue the tufts to the B spaces on the mask. Glue the C and D areas on the quills to the back of the mask so the outlines match up evenly. Make sure to cut the dark lines above the eyes so the eyes pop out.

Mouse Deer Costumes

The mouse deer is a furred animal so the layering technique used for the seal's fur on page 10 can be applied to this mask and breastplate as well. The colours used for the mouse deer costume should be golds and browns.

Cut the dark line at the side of the ears. Fold along the fold line. Glue the glue tab behind the ear (behind the dot of the fold line) to make the ear bend.

The Tiger's Whisker

The Tiger King is pacing back and forth across the stage. Three Tiger Advisers watch him.

Tiger King: I have sent tigers all over the island in search of food and they come back with nothing. What can I do? I have a responsibility to my subjects! They're going to starve. You're my advisers. What do you suggest I do?

The three Tiger Advisers converse among themselves.

Tiger King: Hurry up! I'm waiting.

Tiger Adviser 1: We must examine the facts of the matter, Your Majesty.

Tiger King: Yes? And what are they?

Tiger Adviser 2: Fact No. 1. There are very few animals left on this island for us to hunt.

Tiger King: Don't waste my time! We know that already!

Tiger Adviser 3: Fact No. 2. There are over 13,000 islands in the Indonesian archipelago, of which this island is only one.

Tiger King: What does it matter to us how many islands there are in the Indonesian archipelago? We're tigers, we can't swim to other islands. And I don't suppose the animals we hunt are going to swim to us.

Tiger Adviser 1 *(with a fake, polite laugh)*: Yes, Your Majesty, that is true. You are, as usual, right in all things. But Your Majesty is so powerful.... Why don't you command someone other than a tiger to make a reconnaissance mission to the nearby islands?

Tiger King: Yes, why don't I?

Tiger Adviser 2: Bring in the Hornbills!

Eight Tiger Officers hustle four Hornbills onto the stage.

Tiger Adviser 3: These are Hornbills, Your Majesty. May we suggest you command each one of them to fly in a different direction. The first to return with information about animals for us to hunt on another island will receive a generous reward—to be

determined by Your Majesty, of course.

Tiger King: Yes, yes! That's good. *(to the Hornbills)* You've heard your instructions. There's no time to waste! My stomach is grumbling! Depart at once!

The Hornbills "fly" off on their reconnaissance mission. After a short interval, one Hornbill runs on-stage and drops onto his knees before the Tiger King.

Hornbill *(out of breath)*: Your Majesty, I have good news. An island not very far from here has an abundance of juicy mouse deer. They could provide food for Your Majesty and your subjects for a long time.

Tiger King: Really? *(He looks around, pleased. The Tiger Advisers and Tiger Officers express their delight.)* Where is this island?

Hornbill: Just to the east.

Tiger King: Is it the island we can see from here?

Hornbill: Yes, Your Majesty.

Tiger Adviser 1: It is close enough, Your Majesty, for us to build a bridge of stones to reach it.

Tiger King: Build the bridge immediately. My officers will carry a message to the king of that island telling him to send food to us immediately. If he refuses, we will invade the island and take what we want for ourselves.

Tiger Advisers and Tiger Officers: Yes, Your Majesty.

The Tiger Advisers and Tiger Officers lay down a series of "stones" for the bridge. To get to the island to the east, the Tiger Officers will hop along from stone to stone.

Tiger King: Is it ready?

Tiger Advisers and Tiger Officers: Yes, Your Majesty.

Tiger King: When you deliver my message, I want you to strike fear into all who listen. Take this whisker of mine with you. I want the king of the island to the east to know how great and powerful I am.

The Tiger King "plucks" one of his whiskers. The Tiger Advisers and Tiger Officers gasp, then sigh with relief when it's clear the Tiger King is not in pain.

Tiger King: Here! Take it!

Tiger Advisers and **Tiger Officers:** Yes, Your Majesty.

The Tiger King and Tiger Advisers exit. The three Tiger Officers make their military-style crossing to the other island with the Hornbill in the lead.

Tiger Officer 1: We're here! But I don't see any inhabitants.

Hornbill: Sssh! Here come some now!

Two Mouse Deer enter.

Mouse Deer 1 *(trying to hide her trembling)*: Hello!

Tiger Officer 1: Greetings! We bring a message from the great Tiger King of the island to the west.

Tiger Officer 2: Where is your king? We must deliver the message directly to him.

Mouse Deer 2 *(looking anxiously at Mouse Deer 1)*: We don't have a king.

Tiger Officer 3: You don't have a king?

Mouse Deer 1 *(nudging Mouse Deer 2)*: What my fellow mouse deer means is we are ruled by a queen not a king.

Tiger Officer 3: All right. Where is your queen?

Mouse Deer 1: She's having a nap.

Tiger Officer 2: Well, wake her up! We must deliver this message to her right away. Where can we find her?

Mouse Deer 1: Our queen will be very angry if you wake her up. She doesn't like strangers. I suggest you let me take the message to her for you.

The three Tiger Officers confer among themselves.

Tiger Officer 3: All right, you may take the message to her for us.

Tiger Officer 1: This is our king's demand. Your queen must send food for all his subjects to his island immediately. If your queen refuses, our king will invade this island.

Mouse Deer 2: Oh, no!

Mouse Deer 1: I will deliver the message to our queen and bring you her answer. Rest here until I return. My friend will bring you some cool coconut milk for refreshment.

Hornbill: I'll come with you.

Mouse Deer 1: You're a bird. It will be difficult for you to run swiftly along the forest paths with me and you won't be able to see me from the air.

Hornbill: That's true.

Mouse Deer 1: Please be patient. I will return immediately.

Tiger Officer 2: All right. We'll wait. But return quickly with your queen's answer.

Mouse Deer 1: I will, I will. Rest in the shade of those trees. *(points off-stage)* I'll bring the answer soon.

Tiger Officer 1: Just one more thing. Our king sent this whisker to show how great and powerful he is. It is from his royal visage. Please take it to your queen along with our message.

Tiger Officer 2: We'll have a look around those rice fields while we're waiting.

The Tiger Officers give Mouse Deer 1 the whisker and with the Hornbill follow Mouse Deer 2 off-stage.

Mouse Deer 1: What am I going to do? If the king

sends his army to invade our island, he will want meat. And *I'm* meat.

Porcupine enters.

Porcupine: Hello, Mouse Deer.

Mouse Deer 1: Hello, Porcupine. I'm so glad you've come. Something terrible has happened! The Tiger King from the island to the west says he will invade our island immediately if we don't send him enough food for him and all his subjects.

Porcupine: What kind of food does he want?

Mouse Deer 1: Meat! Meat! Tigers eat meat. To a tiger I'm lunch and dinner. *(brandishing the whisker)* This is the Tiger King's whisker.

Porcupine *(trembling)*: It looks as if it came from a very large tiger.

Mouse Deer 1: It sure does. *(She shivers.)*

Porcupine: What are you going to do?

Mouse Deer 1: I don't know. At least you've got weapons. *(She looks enviously at Porcupine's quills.)* Hmmm ... that gives me an idea. Will you give me one of your longest quills?

Porcupine: Of course. I'll help you in any way I can. *(He reaches behind his back and pulls out his longest quill.)* Here you go. What are you going to do with it?

Mouse Deer 1 *(measuring the quill against the whisker)*: You tell me, Porcupine. If this is from a great Tiger King *(holding up the whisker)*, how large a creature would you say *this* is from *(holding up the quill)*?

Porcupine: A very large one! You're so clever!

Mouse Deer 1: Let me go and get rid of these three brave tigers from the island to the west.

Porcupine *(while exiting)*: Good luck!

Mouse Deer 2 *(running in from the opposite direction)*: Mouse Deer! Watch out! They're coming! They wouldn't wait any longer.

The Tiger Officers and the Hornbill enter from the same direction as Mouse Deer 2.

Tiger Officer 1: Well, Mouse Deer! Did you deliver the message?

Mouse Deer 1: Yes! Yes, I did.

Tiger Officer 2: What was your queen's response? Tell us immediately.

Mouse Deer 1: Our queen sends greetings to the Tiger King of the island to the west.

Tiger Officer 1: As she should.

Tiger Officer 2: What else did she say?

Mouse Deer 1: She regrets that she must tell you she is

unable to send your king any food.

Tiger Officer 3: What?

Tiger Officer 2: How dare she? Did you give her our king's whisker? Didn't she see how mighty he is?

Mouse Deer 1: Yes, of course I gave her the whisker. Our queen likes to receive presents. She also likes to give them. She would like to give this to your king in return.

Mouse Deer 1 hands the quill to Tiger Officer 3.

Tiger Officer 3: What's this?

Mouse Deer 1: It's one of our queen's whiskers.

Tiger Officer 2: But it's so large!

Mouse Deer 1 *(laughing)*: Our queen has many whiskers larger than that one.

The Tiger Officers and the Hornbill look at one another in fear.

Tiger Officer 1: Please excuse us. We must return to our island immediately.

Mouse Deer 2 *(very sweetly)*: Are you sure you wouldn't like some more coconut milk?

Tiger Officer 2: No! No! We're afraid not. We're in a hurry. Goodbye, Mouse Deer.

The Tiger Officers and the Hornbill exit in a hurry across the stone bridge.

Mouse Deer 1: *(laughing)* That scared them off. They won't come here again.

Mouse Deer 2: You're a genius!

Tiger Mask

Tiger Whiskers, Eyebrows, Ears, and Nose

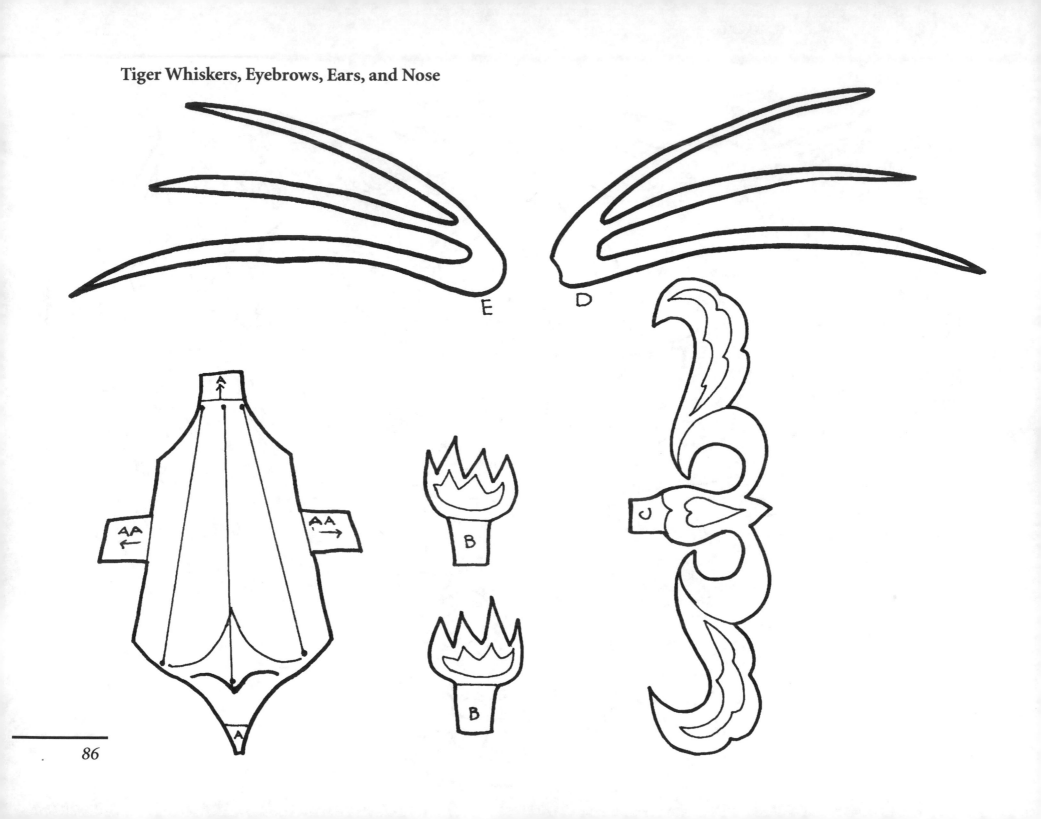

E   D

AA   AA

B

B

C

Tiger Breastplate

Tiger Breastplate

Glue

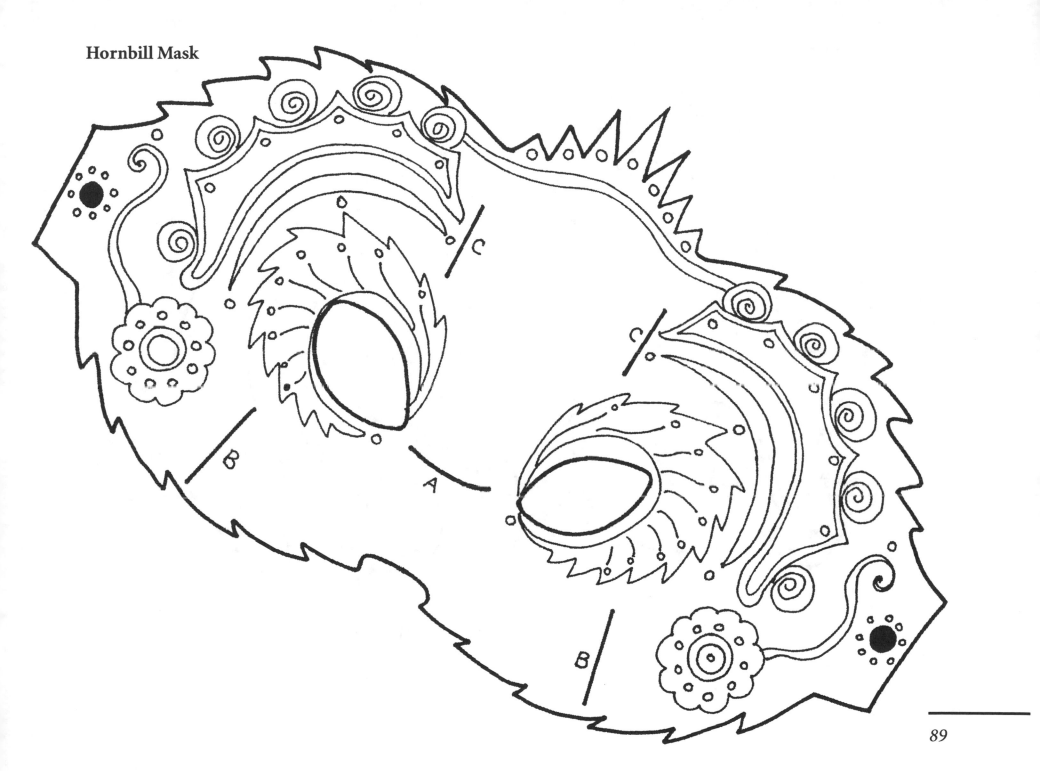

Hornbill Mask

89

Hornbill Bulge

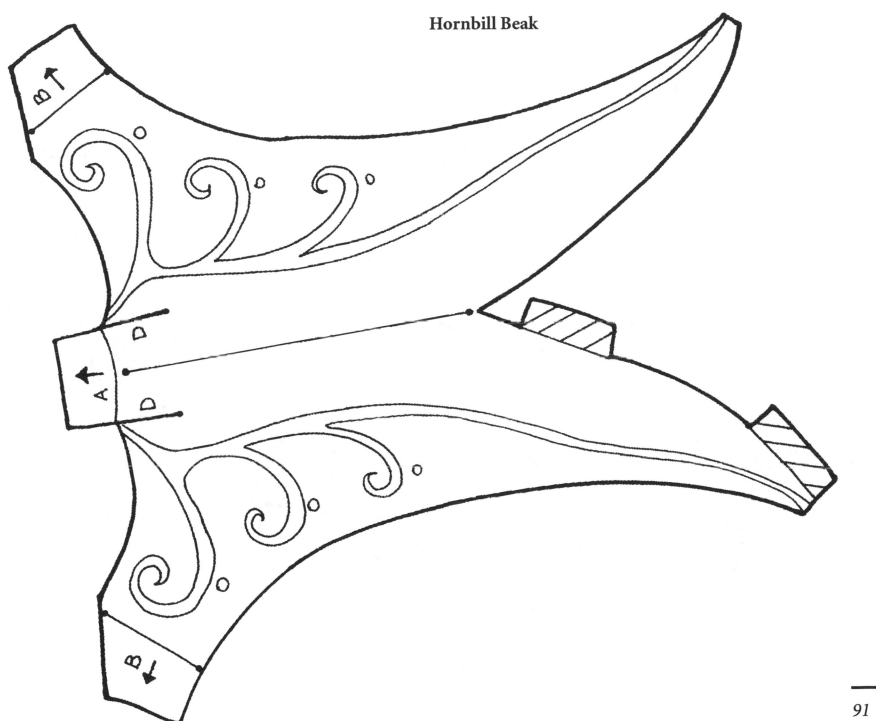

Hornbill Beak

Hornbill Breastplate

Hornbill Breastplate

Porcupine Mask

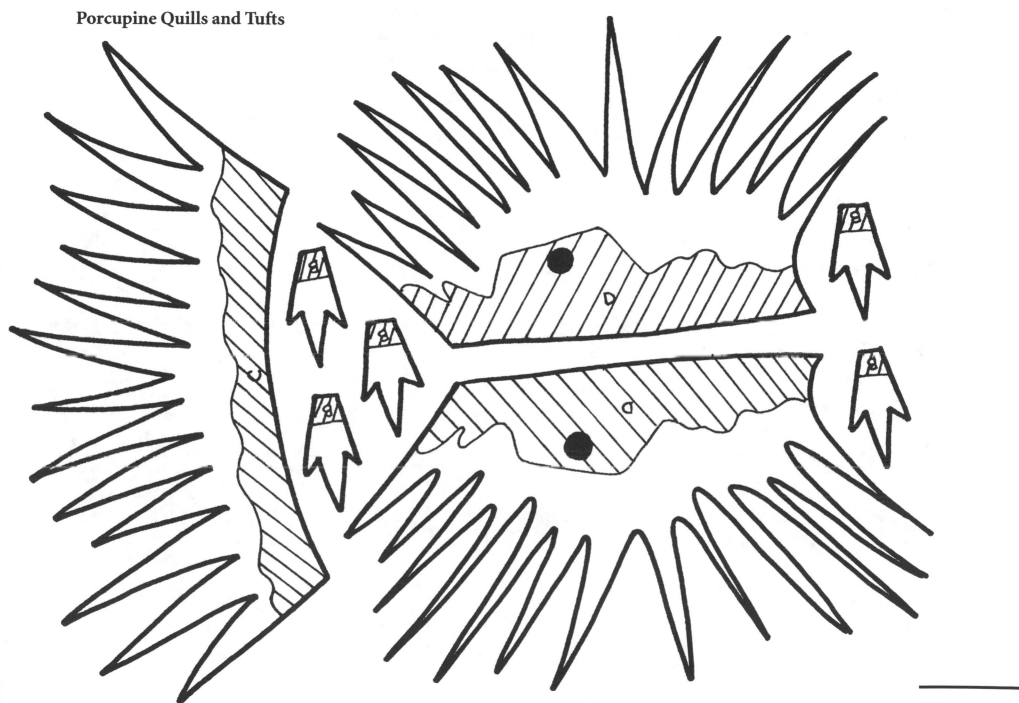

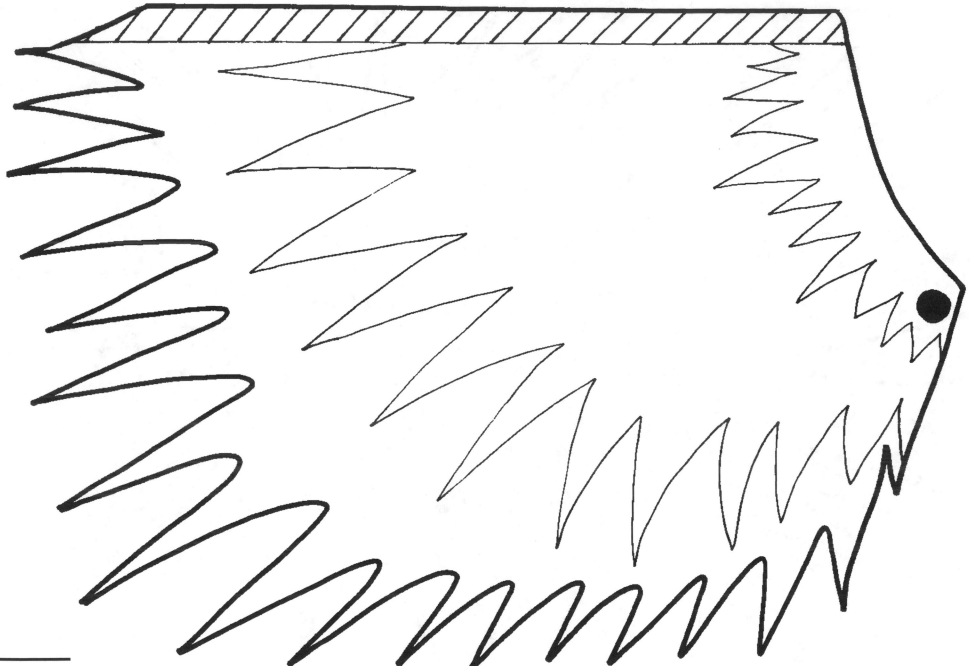

Porcupine Breastplate

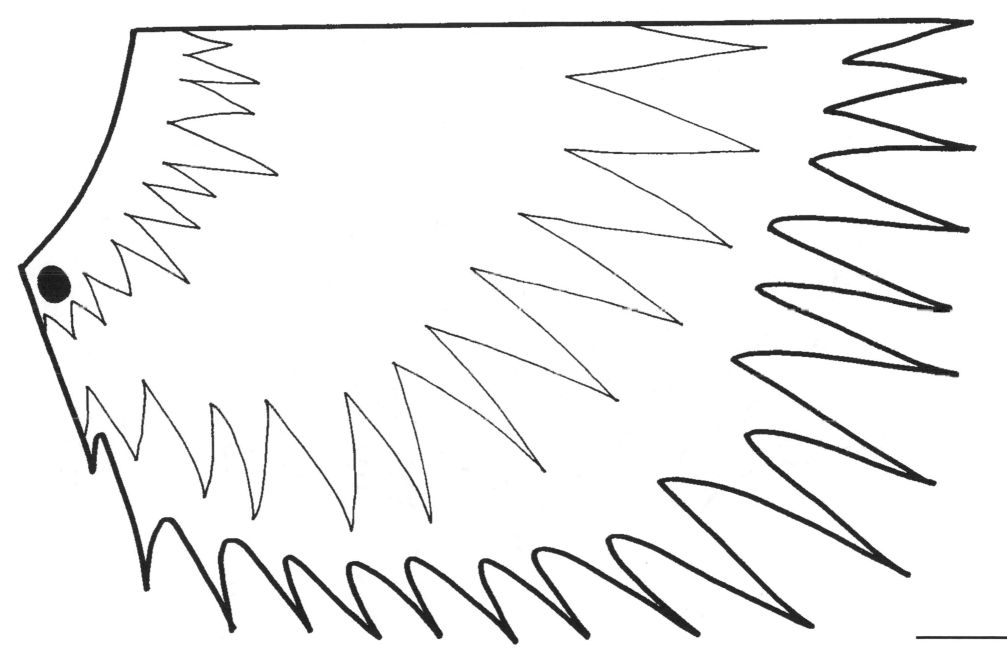

**Mouse Deer Mask
and Ears**

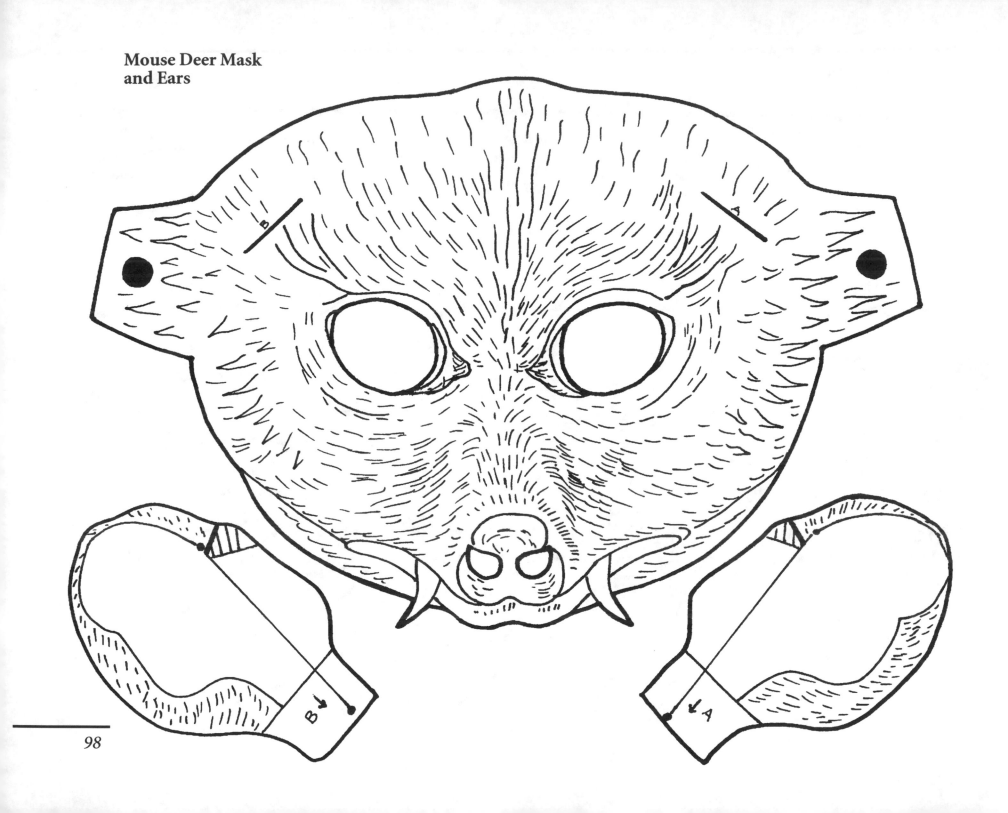

98

Mouse Deer Breastplate

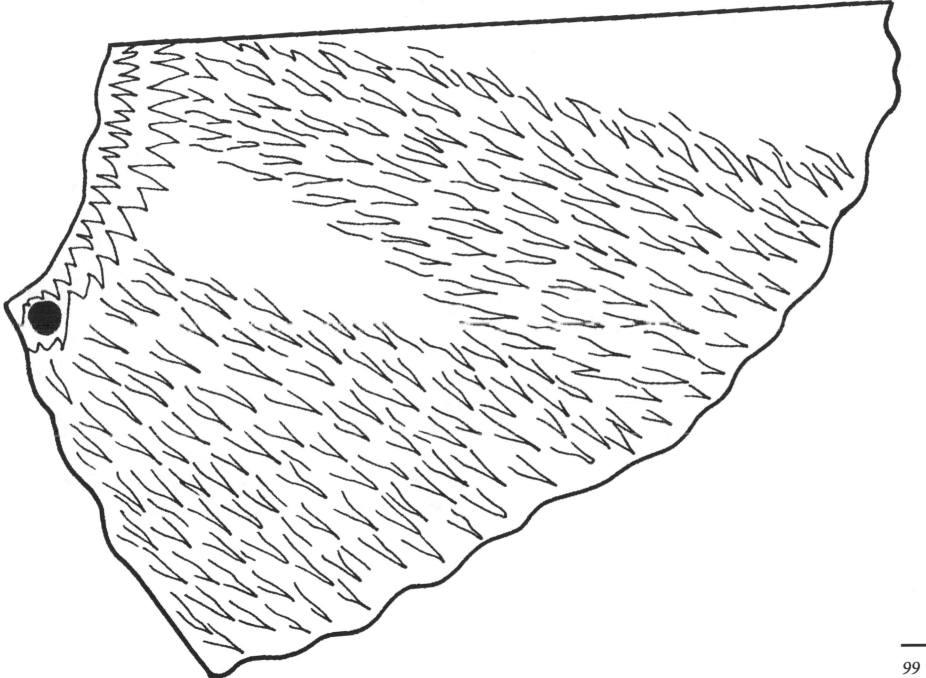

Mouse Deer Breastplate

100

Activities

Retelling Indonesian Legends
Background Information

Some of Indonesia's many legends and tales are creation myths. Most of the legends involve Indonesian gods and goddesses, some of them of Hindu origin, and some more ancient deities, like Dewi Sri, the rice goddess and her husband Wisnu who flies everywhere on his magic bird, the Garuda. These older gods and goddesses have been incorporated into Indonesian Hinduism. The Balinese also have tales about Saraswati, their river goddess, and Sirva, their mountain god. On Java, where Islam is practised in addition to Hinduism, the tales are different and are dominated by stories about Islamic princes and princesses. While the legends of Java and Bali can be quite different, both islands have legends about the creator spirit who resides in volcanoes. On Java this spirit is called Bromo and is believed to live in the mountain named after it. On Bali the volcano spirit, a female, is believed to reside at Bali's holy mountain, *Gunung Agung*. The Balinese call *Gunung Agung* the "navel of the world." *Gunung Agung* is the site of the most famous of Bali's temples, *Besakih*, the Mother Temple. Every village in Bali has its own shrine at *Besakih* where families can leave offerings of rice, rice wine, fruit, and flower petals. The offerings are left to keep the gods and goddesses happy and to ensure that the world is a place of harmony.

Activity

Your group may want to read a legend and retell it in their own words, perhaps as a picture book to which they could contribute their various skills as illustrators and writers. Two children's books which provide a wealth of Indonesian tales are:

Knappert, Jan. *Myths and Legends of Indonesia.* Singapore, Kuala Lumpur, Hong Kong: Heinemann Educational Books, 1977.

Koutsoukis, Albert, Translator. *Indonesian Folk Tales.* Adelaide and Sydney: Rigby, 1970.

Creating a Javanese Puppet Play
Background Information

Java's puppet plays, *wayang golek*, are considered the "soul" of Java. Through them, the Javanese, a reverent people who believe strongly in the importance of manners and respect for one another, use *wayang golek* to teach their children the values of self-control and self-sacrifice.

Wayang golek preserves ancient Javanese beliefs that pre-date the introduction of Islam in the fifteenth century. Most commonly, *wayang golek* tells stories from the Hindu epics the *Ramayana* and the *Mahabarata*, but *wayang golek* is much older than even Indonesian Hinduism. *Wayang golek* preserves the magical relationship between the people of the island and the *dukun*, the shamanistic figure who acted as a messenger between the world of the gods and the world of the Javanese. The most important person in *wayang golek* is the *dalang*, who is very like the *dukun*. The *dalang* writes the scripts, works the puppets, and conducts the *gamelan* orchestra; but most importantly the *dalang* is regarded as the magical figure who breathes life into his puppets. Unlike other Asian puppet-plays, *wayang golek* are shadow plays. They involve a screen, a lamp, and finely-crafted, ornate puppets, which are flat and made of leather. The puppet plays sometimes go on all night.

Activity

Your group could take a hands-on approach to learning more about Javanese culture by producing their own shadow puppet play based on a Javanese legend or folk tale. Simple, two-dimensional puppets could be made out of cardboard and manipulated from above by way of strings or from below (if the screen is high) by mounting the puppets on sticks. Any translucent piece of cloth or paper will work as a screen.

Sharing Trickster Stories
Background Information

In "The Tiger's Whisker," the mouse deer tricks the tigers into thinking the porcupine's quill is a whisker from the queen's face. Many cultures have a similar trickster character in their folk tales. Examples include Coyote from North America, Ananse the Spider from West Africa and the Caribbean, Hare or Rabbit from many countries in southeast Asia, and Raven from the Pacific Northwest coast of North America. The most intriguing aspect of these trickster figures is their ability to transform themselves into another animal or bird and sometimes a person in order to work their deceptions.

Reading some of these trickster tales provides you with the opportunity to note similarities between cultures. With Coyote and Raven it is also an opportunity to explore origin myths. There are many North American First Nations myths about the attempts of Raven and Coyote to steal fire and the sun and the moon. In many of these stories, the sun and the moon are in a box that Raven and Coyote, full of curiosity, cannot resist opening before they have safely reached their destination—and the sun and the moon escape to take their places in the sky. A special type of trickster tale involves the perennial and famous trickster figure from a particular culture being outsmarted—for once—by another creature who proves a little more sharp-witted.

Activity

Encourage your group to tell trickster tales from their own cultures or invite parents or community members to class to share trickster tales. Your group could also choose to write a play script from one or more of these trickster tales. If your group breaks into smaller groups, each one could read a different trickster tale and turn it into a simple play script that they could then present as a staged reading for the other groups. This is a good way to introduce the group as a whole to several trickster tales, after which their similarities and differences can be explored in discussion. You can find a wealth of trickster tales for children in the following books:

Appiah, Peggy. *Ananse the Spider: Tales from an Ashanti Village*. New York: Pantheon Books, 1966.

Greene, Jonathan. *Trickster Tales*. Minneapolis: Coffee House Press, 1985.

Kaula, Edna Maso. *African Village Folktales*. Cleveland: The World Publishing Company, 1968.

Robinson, Gail, Douglas Hill, and Peter Stevenson. *Coyote the Trickster: Legends of the North American Indians*. London: Piccolo Books, 1981.

Robinson, Gail. *Raven the Trickster: Legends of the North American Indians*. London: Chatto & Windus, 1981.

Sherlock, Philip. *Anansi the Spider Man: Jamaican Folk Tales*. New York: Thomas Y. Cromwell, 1954.

Making a Tempera Paper Batik

For background information on batiks, your group can read **Art Master 3**. Invite each member of your group to choose an animal, bird, or butterfly from Indonesia they would like to use as an image for their batik. Choices may include the komodo dragon, orangutan, leaf monkey, gibbon, green turtle, barking deer, peacock, mouse deer, slow loris, the bird of paradise, the dwarf buffalo of Sulawesi, the one-horned rhinoceros of Java, or the fresh water snake that inhabits the terraced wet-rice fields of Bali and is venerated as the rice goddess Dewi Sri. Your group can research the shapes of the creature they have chosen and their environments using encyclopedias, geography magazines, and traveller's guide books as well as books specifically on the topic. They can then sketch the designs or symbols they would like to use to decorate their batik creature. **Art Master 3** provides further suggestions on how to do this as well as instructions on how to complete a tempera paper batik.

Learning about Spices

Background Information

The use of spices has a long history. Spices were used as a flavouring and preservative agent long before refrigeration was invented. They were also used for medicinal purposes. Many early European expeditions were sent out in search of spices and much of the early interest in Indonesia, initially by the Portuguese and later by the Dutch, centred on the spice trade, especially in pepper, nutmeg, and mace. The spice industry is still very important to Indonesia.

Activity

There are many spices and they are used in many different ways. Your group could interview whoever does the cooking in their homes to find out which spices are used in their food. They could bring samples of spices and herbs to share with others in the group. Or your group could research a variety of spices and herbs. Divide the children into small groups and have each group make a "spice and herb poster" using either real samples, which can be attached to the poster with glue or clear tape, or photographs or drawings of the plant. They can use the poster to give an oral report to others explaining the names, origins, and uses of the spices/herbs. Students could use **Research Master 3** to guide their research.

Finding Out About Balinese Mask Dramas

Background Information

The Balinese are famous for the colourful, elaborate masks they use in their traditional dramas, processions, and dance rituals. These masks are called *tapel.* The wood they are made from is often consecrated before it is carved because it is believed that the spirit it represents will enter it during a performance of the mask drama. Mask carvers use many different materials in the masks to make them elegant and ornate. The Balinese masks often make use of the teeth of wild pigs, horse hair, buffalo hides, and rabbit pelts, as well as ornamental materials like gold leaf, jewels, mirrors, and coins.

The masks depict humans, animals, divinities, and demons, and it is believed that they summon supernatural entities to take part in and watch the dramas and rituals. Many of the stories behind the Balinese mask dramas are drawn from the Hindu *Ramayana* and *Mahabarata.* Balinese Hinduism is distinct from Indian Hinduism, however, and the stories have been adapted to suit Balinese beliefs.

Begun around 1000 C.E. as an entertainment sponsored by kings, in the twentieth century the Balinese mask dramas are mounted and financed by community groups called *banjar,* one of which is found in every Balinese neighbourhood. The playing space is always outside. Spectators either sit on the ground or stand. Called the *kalagan,* the playing space is blessed by a priest before a performance takes place. There are no sets *per se,* but sometimes foliage or carved palm leaves are used to decorate the playing area.

One of the most popular Balinese mask dramas is the *Barong Ket.* The Barong Ket is a lion spirit who is believed to be the head of the forces of white magic. The Balinese are reluctant to think in terms of good and evil because they do not believe that the two are easily separated; any person or spirit, depending on how they are influenced, can act in a positive, creative way or in a negative, destructive one. The *Barong Ket* stages a ritualistic battle between creative forces, led by Barong Ket, and between nihilistic forces, led by Rangda, the Goddess of Death. The dancers who represent creative forces wear Barong masks, and those who represent destructive forces wear Rangda masks. At the drama's climax, Rangda and her demons appear to be winning; with her magic, she forces the Barong dancers to turn their daggers (called *krisses*) upon themselves. This part of the drama is called the *ngurek.* It is believed that when they are performing the *ngurek,* the Barong dancers go into trance. In the trance, their ancestor spirits enter their bodies and the strength of the spirits keeps the *krisses* from doing them any harm. The *Barong Ket* is performed as a purifying ritual for the community, which exorcises their negative, destructive energy.

Activity

Students could research the different kinds of Balinese masks and learn the stories behind the characters that the masks portray. They could show pictures of their masks and give oral presentations to the group. Balinese masks have been influenced by other Asian cultures, so students could also research similar masks from Java, Sumatra, Nepal, and Sri Lanka.

---

* during the Christian era

Batik and Batik Designs

"Batik" means "little drops" and refers to the little drops of wax used to make patterns on fabric. A high quality batik takes several months to complete because the designs must be drawn with hot wax identically on both sides of the fabric. Hot wax is used to draw designs on fabric, and when the fabric is dyed, the areas of wax do not absorb the colour.

No one is sure where the art of batik originated, but by the thirteenth century it was a highly developed art form in Indonesia. At one time, certain designs were restricted and only members of the nobility could wear them.

Indonesian batik designs have their origins in Arabic, Indian, and Chinese art and are often based on flowers, animals, and birds. Some designs, like the *Kawung*, are based on geometric patterns. Bird designs include the Garuda, rooster, and peacock. The Garuda is a bird from Indian mythology; sometimes the whole bird appears in the design, sometimes it is represented by a pair of wings, and sometimes even by a single wing. The rooster is the symbol of the sun and bravery.

Some examples of designs used in batik are shown on this page.

Making A Paper Batik

You will need:
- a large sheet of heavyweight construction paper in a light shade of grey, blue, pink, yellow, or brown
- liquid tempera paint in various bright colours and black tempera paint
- white chalk
- paint brushes
- a sheet of hard plastic larger than the paper

Follow these steps:
1. Draw a large outline of your animal with the white chalk, then use the chalk to fill the interior of the animal with symbols and designs.
2. Paint the animal, symbols, and designs, but leave the chalk lines unpainted. Let the painting dry completely.
3. Use a soft cloth to wipe off any excess chalk.
4. Mix a diluted wash of black tempera paint and use a wide brush to cover the painting lightly with it. Let the painting dry completely.
5. Place the painting on the sheet of plastic and run cold water over it—for a *few seconds* only so the design does not wash away. Gently sponge off any excess water. Once again, let the painting dry completely.
6. Coat the painting with a clear varnish.

Researching Spices and Herbs

Choose one spice or herb to research. Jot down information about the spice or herb under the following headings.

The herb or spice I have chosen is: _____

1. In which parts of the world does the herb or spice grow?	2. What kind of climate and growing conditions does your plant prefer?
3. How is the spice or herb used by people? Is it used only in cooking?	4. What other interesting facts about the herb or spice did you discover?

The Hare's Liver

About the Play

"The Hare's Liver" is based on a Korean folk tale. A hare is tricked into accompanying a turtle to the bottom of the sea where the sea dragon king lives. The sea dragon king is going to have the hare killed so he can eat her liver to save his own life. The particular folk tale from which this play is drawn makes use of a common folk tale theme, travel into a world that represents the world of the dead. In this case, the heroine, by using her wits, is able to make the journey and return alive—and intact!

Korea's geographic location on a peninsula between the East China Sea and the Sea of Japan has caused it to have a troubled history over the last several thousand years. Caught between China and Japan, Korea has been invaded by both countries many times, and has often been the battleground for Chinese and Japanese aggression against one another. As a result, Korea has been influenced by both Chinese and Japanese culture, but it too has influenced those cultures in turn. Korea's folk tales reflect over three thousand years of cultural exchange that began, according to legend, when Kija, a Chinese wise man, led several thousand followers out of China and into the Korean peninsula. With its history, it is easy to understand why this folk tale about a small creature who is able to outwit a large, powerful aggressor has enduring popularity with Koreans.

After World War II, Japan's most recent occupation of Korea ended and Korea was split in two. North Korea adopted a Communist government under the influence of China. South Korea adopted a more Western style of government. However, people in both countries have worked hard to preserve and maintain their shared cultural heritage.

The following are some sources for further information about Korean folklore:

Hung Ha, Tae. *Folk Tales of Old Korea.* Seoul: Yonsi University Press, 1958; ninth printing, 1984.

In-Sob, Zong. *Folk Tales from Korea.* Seoul: Hollym International Corp., 1952; third edition, 1982.

Korean Cultural Studies Society. *The Morning Bright.* Seoul: Ewha Woman's University Press, 1990.

Shin-Yong, Chun, general editor. *Korean Folk Tales.* Translated by Lee Tae-Dong and Dolores Geier. Seoul: International Cultural Foundation, 1979.

So-un, Kim. *The Story Bag: A Collection of Korean Folktales.* Translated by Setsu Higashi. Rutland and Tokyo: Charles E. Tuttle Co., 1955; twelfth printing, 1981.

Suggestions for Performing the Play

General information on play performance can be found on pages 5-7. "The Hare's Liver" takes approximately 12 minutes to perform. This time could be extended by adding Korean folk dancing to the party scene that opens the play. The play has 11 speaking parts. You can increase the number of non-speaking parts by having as many fish courtiers as you like. You can also provide the sketch artist with several assistants. These assistants can hand the sketch artist the materials he or she needs to pretend to make the hare portrait, one or two could hold the sketch pad, and another could provide the sketch artist with a chair.

The play has two different settings, the Kingdom at the Bottom of the Sea and land. The action on land should take place in the area closest to the audience. You could use blue gym mats to represent the ocean and the Kingdom at the Bottom of the Sea. This would be a very effective way to make clear distinctions between the play's two settings.

At the close of the second scene and in the last scene, the turtle carries the hare on his back through the water. To show this, the turtle could stoop over, the hare could drape herself over his back, and they could continue in unison. The turtle's movements should be slow and the actors can have some fun experimenting with different ways to "swim." Since turtles flop onto land, your group could also propose a way that the turtle could "flop" onto land in the final scene. Your group might want to exaggerate this, to play up the humour. If you use blue gym mats for the water, the actor playing the hare could also have some fun pretending to tumble off turtle when he flops onto land. For the journey that takes places between Scenes 2 and 3, if you are using a stage, the turtle and the hare can move off-stage and then re-enter from the wings furthest from the audience. If you are not using a stage, have the turtle and the hare travel across the front of the playing area then circle back, along the side of the playing area, to return to the central playing space from the rear.

There are many places in the play where the humour could be emphasized. One is where the fish officials are reading their large hare books. Each one is racing to find the information before the others do. One good way to emphasize the humour of the race would be to have all three of them turn their pages in unison. "The Hare's Liver" has been written to have a special appeal for younger audience members, who are encouraged to contribute to the performance when the turtle goes on his hare-hunting mission and addresses the audience directly.

Suggestions for Scenery, Props, Costumes, and Music

Scenery

If you are using a stage for your performance of "The Hare's Liver," your group could make a sea collage as a backdrop for the play. Please see this chapter's activities section for ideas and instructions on this collage. The land scene could consist of a few trees or bushes that could be moved onto the stage or into the area at the appropriate times. The most common trees in Korea's coastal areas are the oak and the laurel, and Korea's most common bush is the flowering camellia. If your group decides they would like to combine these ideas and prepare a collage of Korean flora for the land scene, they might want to consult the information about Korean calligraphy and painting that can also be found in this chapter's activities section. Traditional Korean painting

has been influenced by the Korean art of calligraphy and uses bold black strokes for its depiction of flora. Your group could easily adopt a similar style for the flora in their collage.

Props

A performance of "The Hare's Liver" requires several props. Each of the fish officials will need a hare book to consult. Your art crew could make mock books, and the entire group could have fun coming up with different titles for each ("Anatomy of a Hare," for example, or "The Complete Hare Book"). The sketch artist will need a sketch pad, of course, but more importantly, a hare portrait needs to be prepared in advance of the performance. The sketch artist will pull this portrait from the sketch pad when it is time to present it to the sea dragon king. You could use the hare mask to create this portrait.

The fish doctor will need a scalpel. This could be made out of cardboard and tinfoil.

Keep in mind that it can add to the humour of the play if all the props are made larger than life.

Costumes

To decorate and assemble the masks and breastplates, follow the general instructions on page 7. For the mouse deer character, please use the mouse deer mask and breastplate from "The Tiger's Whisker." They can be found on pages 98-100. Directions for decorating and assembling the mouse deer costume can be found on page 79. You may also use this furred mouse deer breastplate for the hare. For the monkey character, please use the monkey mask and breastplate that can be found on pages 37-39 of "The Gharial and the Monkey." Directions for decoration and assembly are on page 26. Also give your group the following specific instructions.

Sea Dragon Costumes

Follow the decorating instructions for the turtle costumes on the dragons as well, although you may wish to extend the colour range you use.

Be careful when cutting out the upper edge of the dragon mouths. You do not want to cut through to the nostrils. Remember to fold along all the fold lines on the ears *before* attaching the ears to the mask. To attach the ears to the dragon mask, fold the ear glue tabs A and C over before gluing to glue spaces A and C on the mask.

When assembling the dragon breastplate, fold along the fold lines *before* gluing the two pieces of the breastplate together.

Hare Costumes

Use pencil or wax crayons in browns, yellows, gold, silver, purples, and white to decorate the hare mask and breastplates. To create a textured effect, layer colours on top of each other. To achieve a light and dark effect, vary the pressure applied to the crayons.

To add the hare ears to the mask, fold along the fold lines before gluing. Put glue on the glue tab and pull the tab of the ear down to the glue to make a "dart." The two ears are different, to give the hare a humorous look.

Turtle Costumes

You may use oil pastels or wax crayons in greens, blues, yellows, and purples, black water-based paint, and one-inch brushes to decorate the turtle costumes. To produce a textured effect, colour the masks with related colours, using as many different tints of the colours as possible. The colours should be layered on top of each other for greater effect, and some areas should be left blank. When the crayon or pastel colouring is complete, brush the mask with the water-based paint and lightly sponge off any excess paint.

Remember to cut out the nostrils on the turtle mask. When cutting, be careful not to cut through to the eye sockets. Also make sure to cut the slots under the eyes to release the eye pockets.

Fish Costumes

Use coloured pieces of tissue paper and Rhoplex® to create multi-coloured fish. The Rhoplex® will cause the tissue paper to "bleed" and create an interesting effect.

To give you a selection to choose from, three pairs of fish lips have been provided. To attach the fish lips of your choice, put glue on glue tabs F on the mask and press the corners of the lips onto the glue to make the lips puff out.

Music

There are two moments in the play that call for music: the play's opening dance music and the royal entrances and exits. There are two types of traditional Korean music, *chong-ak,* music for the nobility, and *sog-ak,* folk music. *Chong-ak* includes banquet and military music, which would work well in a performance of "The Hare's Liver."

The Hare's Liver

Scene 1. *The play opens in the Sea Dragon King's Palace on the ocean floor. A royal party is taking place. There is music. As the play begins, the Fish Courtiers are bowing before the Sea Dragon King and Queen who are clapping.*

Sea Dragon Queen: Wasn't that a wonderful performance?

Sea Dragon King: Wonderful!

The Sea Dragon King suddenly cries out in pain.

Sea Dragon Queen: What's the matter?

Sea Dragon King: I don't know. I have a horrible pain in my stomach.

Sea Dragon Queen: Somebody call the King's doctor!

Doctor Fish hurries on-stage.

Doctor Fish: Please, please! Give His Majesty room! I must examine him.

Doctor Fish gently prods the Sea Dragon King's stomach.

Sea Dragon King: Ouch!

Doctor Fish: Hmmm.

Doctor Fish prods another spot.

Sea Dragon King: Ouch! What are you trying to do, make my pain worse?

Doctor Fish: Your Majesty, I'm afraid I have some bad news.

Sea Dragon Queen: Oh, no! Nobody's allowed to give the Sea Dragon King bad news, especially about his health. The Sea Dragon King will live forever!

Sea Dragon King: What is it, Doctor?

Doctor Fish: It's a disease so rare I don't even know the name for it. It affects only Sea Dragons. And there is only one cure.

Sea Dragon King: What is this cure? Tell me at once.

Doctor Fish: Your Majesty, as soon as possible you must eat a boiled hare's liver.

Sea Dragon Queen: A boiled hare's liver!

Fish Courtiers and Officials (*to their nearest neighbours, astonished*): A hare's liver!

Sea Dragon Queen: What's a hare?

Three Fish Officials run on-stage with large books through which they flip hurriedly.

Fish Official 1 (*reading from his book*): Your Majesty, the hare is a creature who lives on land.

Sea Dragon King: A great many creatures live on land. We need more details.

Fish Official 2 (*reading from her book*): Your Majesty, the hare has four fin-like things called paws.

Sea Dragon King: I need to be able to picture this hare creature! Where's my sketch artist?

The Sketch Artist enters with assistants who carry the Sketch Artist's supplies.

Fish Sketch Artist: Here, Your Majesty.

Sea Dragon King: Have you heard? We need to find one of these hare creatures.

Fish Sketch Artist: Yes, Your Majesty.

Sea Dragon King: I need you to draw me a portrait.

Fish Sketch Artist: At once, Your Majesty.

Sea Dragon Queen: Tell the Sketch Artist what we know so far.

Fish Official 2: It has four fin-like things call paws.

The Sketch Artist draws.

Fish Official 3 (*reading from her book*): Your Majesty, the hare has two pink eyes.

The Sketch Artist draws, then pauses, waiting for more information.

Fish Official 1 (*reading from his book*): Your Majesty, the hare has two ears which look like cuttlefish.

The Sketch Artist draws some more.

Sea Dragon King: Good, good! Do we know anything else about the hare?

Fish Official 3 (*reading from her book*): Your Majesty, the hare's body is covered with a mottled brown material called fur.

The Fish Courtiers and the Fish Officials make a collective expression of disgust. The Sketch Artist sketches quickly.

Sea Dragon King: Is the portrait complete?

Fish Sketch Artist: Yes, Your Majesty.

The Sketch Artist turns the portrait round first to the Sea Dragon King, then to the audience. On the sketch pad is a hare body topped with a replica of the hare mask Ms. Hare will wear. The Fish Courtiers and the Fish Officials all clap in delight.

Sea Dragon King: Wonderful! Someone must set out at once in search of this creature. Find a hare and bring it to me!

Fish Official 2: Your Majesty, how are we going to catch a hare? None of us can live out of water.

Sea Dragon King: Then find someone who can.

The Fish Courtiers and Fish Officials look at one another in dismay. The Turtle enters and moves slowly across the stage.

Fish Courtiers and Officials (*to their nearest neighbours*): A turtle! A turtle!

Turtle: Good day, Your Majesties. Good day, everyone.

Sea Dragon Queen: Oh, Turtle! You couldn't have arrived at a better moment!

Fish Official 3: Turtle, you can live out of water, can't you?

Turtle: Yes, that's true. I spend half my time in the water and half my time out of it.

Fish Courtiers and Officials (*to their nearest neighbours*): He can get it! He's our hero!

Turtle (*looking around perplexed*): Your hero?

Sea Dragon King: Turtle, I have a very important mission for you. I have never given any of my fish such an important mission. I want you to go on land at once and bring me back a hare's liver.

Turtle: I don't understand, Your Majesty. Why do you want a hare's liver?

Doctor Fish: We need a fresh hare's liver to cure the King.

The Sea Dragon King cries out in pain.

Sea Dragon Queen: It's our only hope.

Turtle: I'd be honoured to serve His Majesty but I have no idea what a hare looks like. In all my travels on land I've never seen one.

Sea Dragon King: Give him the portrait of the hare.

The Fish Sketch Artist gives the Turtle the hare portrait.

Sea Dragon King: The pain! Oh, the pain! Go, and go quickly! While you're gone we'll decide on your reward.

Turtle: Very well, Your Majesty. I'll do my best to find you a hare.

Fish Official 3: We fish will go with you as far as the ocean's surface.

Ceremonial music. The Sea Dragon King and Queen exit one way, the Fish Courtiers, Fish Officials and Turtle the other.

Scene 2. *On land.*

Turtle: What a beautiful day for a hare-hunting mission.

Monkey walks across the stage.

Monkey: Good day, Turtle.

Turtle: Good day! *(to audience)* Is this a hare? He has four fin-like things. *(to Monkey)* Excuse me one moment. *(Turtle unrolls the portrait. He looks at the portrait, then at Monkey, then back at the portrait.)* Are you a hare?

Monkey: A hare? Of course not! I'm a monkey. And, if you don't mind, I'm in a hurry. I'm hunting for oranges.

Monkey exits.

Turtle *(rolling up his portrait)*: This may be more difficult than I thought.

Mouse Deer enters.

Mouse Deer: Good day, Turtle.

Turtle: Good day. *(to audience)* She has two pink eyes! Excuse me one moment. *(Turtle unrolls the portrait. He looks at the portrait, then at Mouse Deer, then back at the portrait.)* I couldn't help but notice that you have two pink eyes. Are you a hare?

Mouse Deer: A hare? Definitely not. I'm a mouse deer. Don't you recognize a mouse deer when you see one? I belong to the ancient order of chevrotains. My ancestors have lived here for millions of years. We look nothing like hares!

Mouse deer exits in a huff.

Turtle *(calling after her)*: I'm sorry. I didn't mean to offend you. *(rolling up his portrait)* I've seen tigers and wolves and bears, and I've seen red deer and pheasants and salamanders. But I have not seen a single hare. And I'm so tired I don't think I can take another step. I think I'll take a little rest.

Turtle sits down. Ms. Hare enters humming.

Hare: Good day, Turtle.

Turtle *(wearily)*: Good day. *(Turtle takes a second look at Ms. Hare and sits up straight. He unrolls the portrait one more time, excitedly.)* Excuse me one moment. I couldn't help but notice that you have two ears like cuttlefish. Are you a hare?

Hare: Ha, ha, ha! Of course I'm a hare. What else would I be?

Turtle: Ms. Hare, I come from the Kingdom at the Bottom of the Sea. I have been sent by the Sea Dragon King to invite you to his palace. His Majesty has long wanted to meet a hare. He has heard that you are unusual and charming creatures. He is planning a banquet in your honour. He would be very pleased if you would accept his invitation.

Hare: The Sea Dragon King! I've heard of him. What an honour. But how can I go to the Kingdom at the Bottom of the Sea? I can't live under water.

Turtle: Don't worry about that. I have special powers. I will take you there and back safely. Climb onto my back.

Hare: All right. I quite like adventures.

Hare "climbs" onto Turtle's back and they "swim" to the Kingdom at the Bottom of the Sea.

Scene 3. *The Sea Dragon King's Palace. The Sea Dragon King is on-stage with the Sea Dragon Queen and Doctor Fish. The Sea Dragon King is writhing in pain.*

Sea Dragon King: Can't somebody do something to ease my pain?

The Fish Officials and Fish Courtiers rush onstage.

Fish Officials and Fish Courtiers *(in unison)*: Your Majesty! We have good news! The Turtle has captured the Hare!

The Turtle and Ms. Hare enter to ceremonial music.

Turtle *(to Ms. Hare)*: Didn't I tell you you would be treated as a special guest? *(to the Sea Dragon King and Queen)* Your Majesties, I present Ms. Hare. *(Turtle nudges Ms. Hare.)* You should bow.

Hare *(bowing)*: Your Majesties, I am very honoured by your invitation to visit the Kingdom at the Bottom of the Sea.

Sea Dragon Queen: I'm afraid the visit may not turn out quite as you expected.

The Sea Dragon King signals to the Fish Officials who grab Ms. Hare.

Sea Dragon King: Ms. Hare, I need your help with a certain matter.

Hare: Your Majesty, I would be happy to help you. But first tell your fish to keep their fins off me.

Sea Dragon King: Release her, Fish.

The Fish Officials release Ms. Hare.

Hare: Thank you. What can I do to help Your Majesty?

Sea Dragon King: I'm sick. In fact I'm very ill. My doctor tells me that unless I take a certain cure I will die. That cannot be allowed to happen! I am a Sea Dragon King and I intend to live forever.

Hare: What is the cure, Your Majesty? Is it something I can get for you?

The Fish Courtiers and Fish Officials titter.

Doctor Fish: There is only one cure, Ms. Hare, and that is fresh hare's liver.

Hare: Fresh hare's liver?

Sea Dragon King: I'm afraid that's why I commanded Turtle to bring you here. I must have your liver.

Hare: My liver!

Sea Dragon King: Please don't think that your sacrifice will go unrewarded. You will be honoured for saving my life. You will have a magnificent funeral, as fine a funeral as I would have if I died—which I refuse to do!

Hare (*with a loud sigh*): Your Majesty, I'm afraid Turtle has gone to a great deal of trouble for nothing. If only Turtle had been honest with me, I could have brought my liver with me.

Fish Courtiers and Officials (*to their neighbours*): Oh, no! She didn't bring her liver with her!

Sea Dragon King: You mean you don't have it with you?

Hare: No, Your Majesty. My liver has special healing powers. Everybody wants it! I have to keep it hidden in a secret cave.

Sea Dragon Queen: Oh, no!

Sea Dragon King: Now I *will* die!

The Sea Dragon King seems to faint. The Fish Courtiers and Fish Officials gasp.

Doctor Fish: Don't despair, Your Majesty. She's lying. No creature can live without a liver. It cleans the poison out of our bodies. I'll cut her open right now if you want. We'll soon find out the truth.

Doctor Fish brandishes a scalpel. The Fish Courtiers and Fish Officials gasp again.

Hare: I'm not lying, Your Majesty. You can have my liver! I would be honoured to give it to you. Command Turtle to take me back to land and I'll get it. But if you cut me open now, I'll die for sure and you'll never get my liver.

The Sea Dragon King motions to the Fish Officials. They huddle around him and hold a whispered consultation.

Sea Dragon King: I have made my decision. Turtle, take Ms. Hare back to land to get her liver and return with it as soon as possible.

Turtle (*bowing*): Yes, Your Majesty.

The Sea Dragon King and Queen and the Fish Courtiers and Officials exit to ceremonial music.

Turtle: Well, let's get going. You heard the Sea Dragon King's command. We have to return as quickly as possible.

Hare: Yes, let's go.

They begin to "swim" back to land.

Hare: Can't you go any faster?

Turtle: As you know, Ms. Hare, turtles are not known for their speed. I'm moving as quickly as I can.

Hare: I can see land!

They "land."

Hare *(leaping free)*: Good-bye, Turtle! Thanks for the ride.

Turtle: Wait a minute! You're supposed to get your liver to give to the Sea Dragon King. He won't be able to live without it.

Hare: Maybe not, but I won't be able to live without it either. And it is my liver, after all. You were foolish, Turtle, and they were all foolish fish, to believe that I would give it up.

Turtle: What am I going to tell the Sea Dragon King?

Hare: The truth! That nobody can live forever, not even a Sea Dragon King!

Hare darts off-stage, and Turtle plods off slowly in the other direction.

Sea Dragon Mask

Sea Dragon Ear and Horn

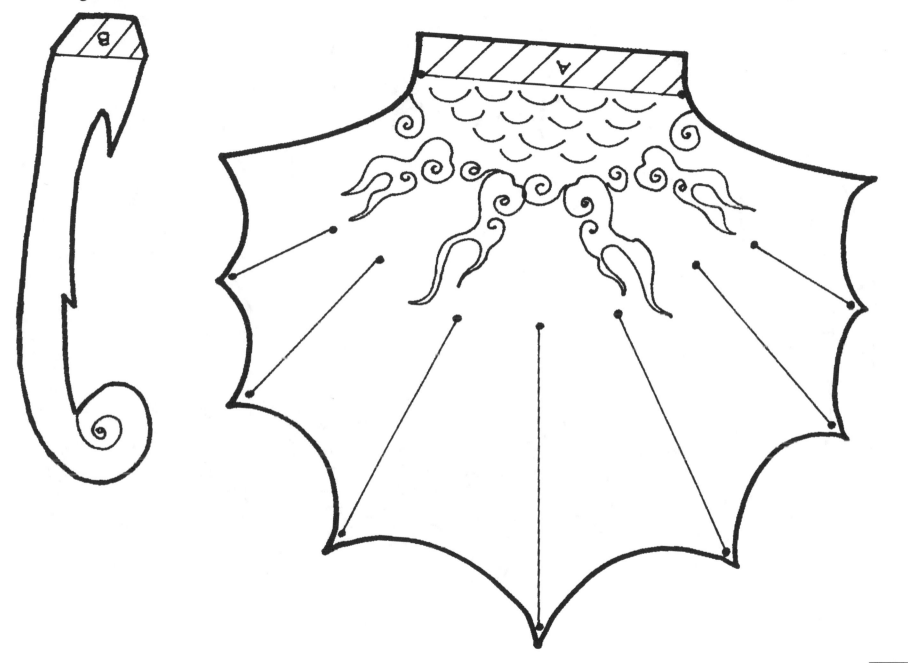

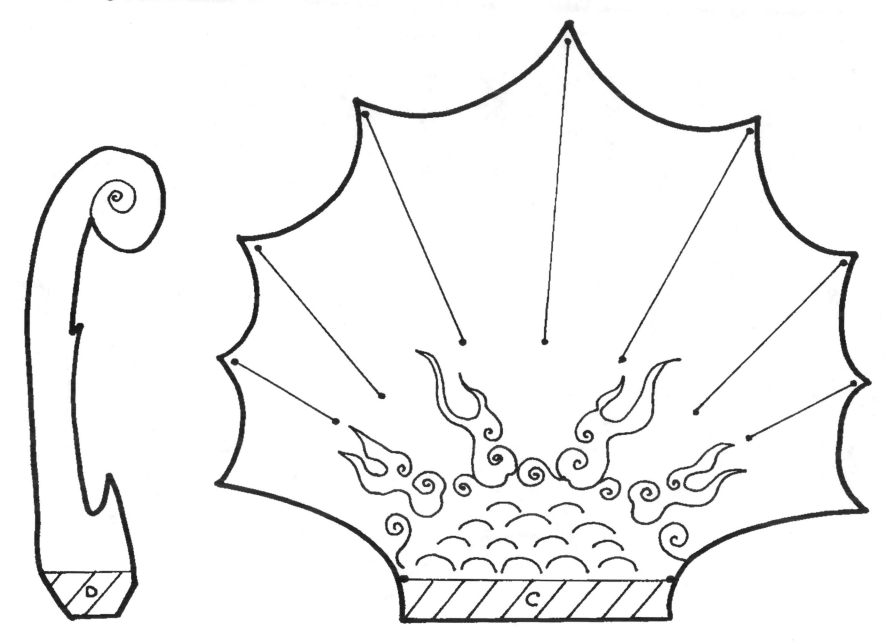

Dragon Breastplate

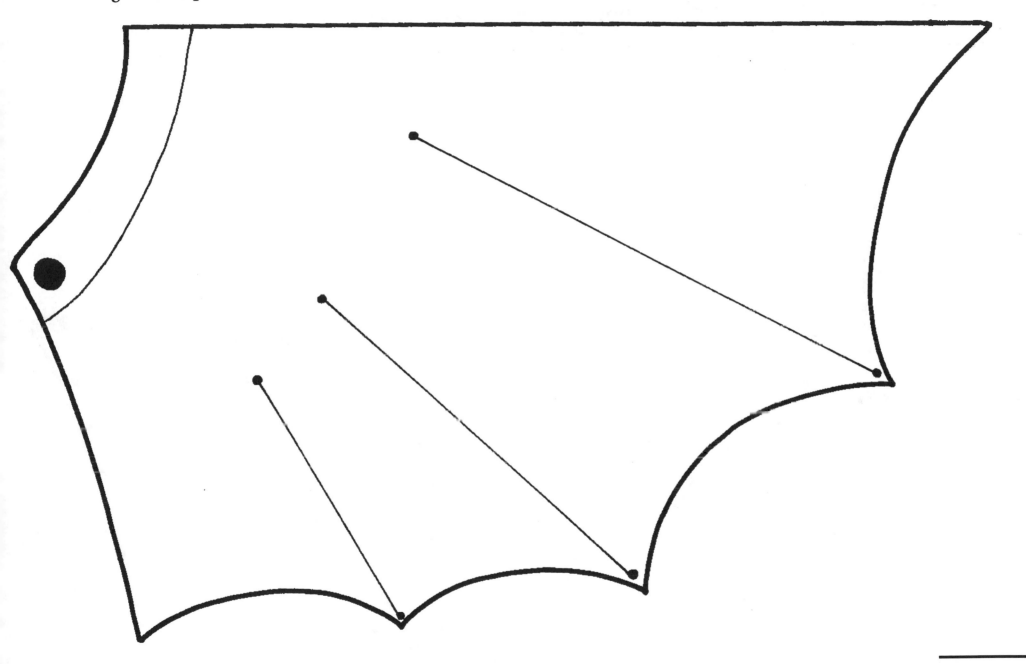

Dragon Breastplate

Hare Mask

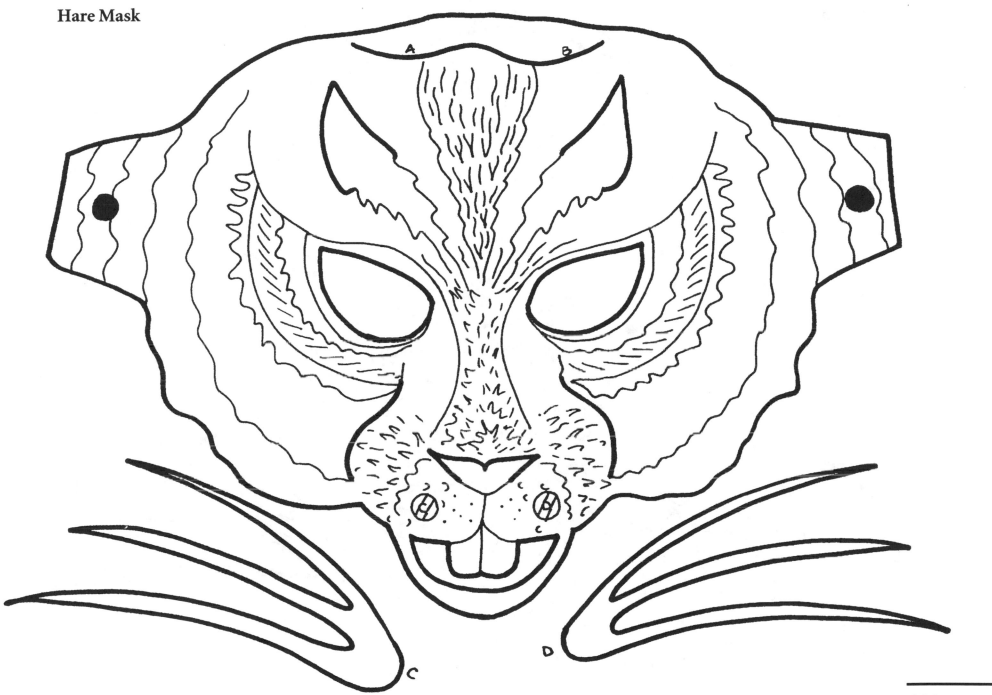

Hare Ears

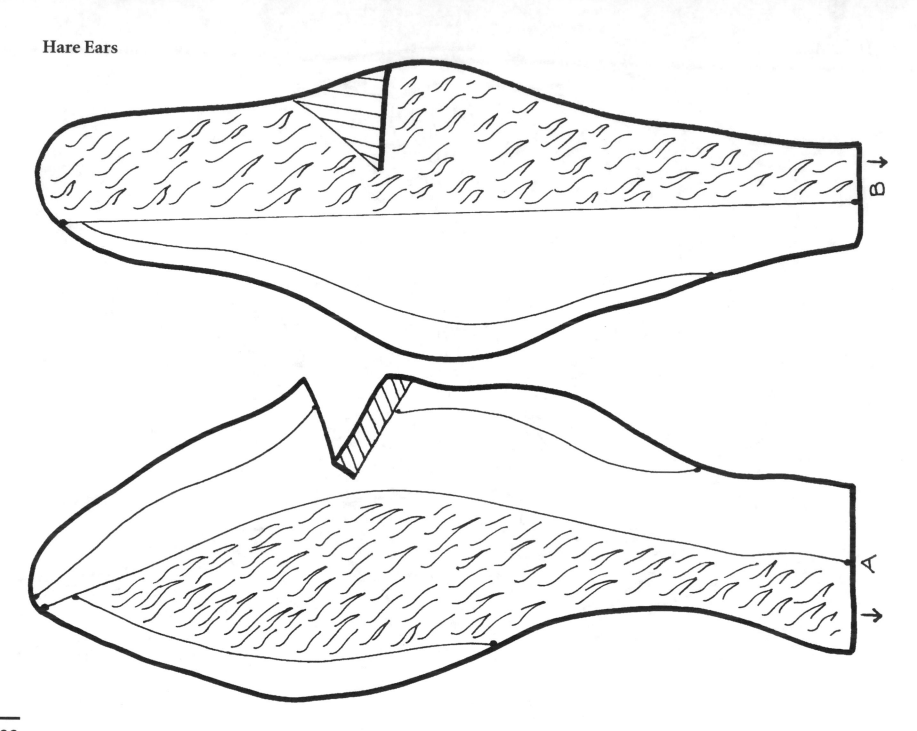

**Turtle Mask and
Eyebrows**

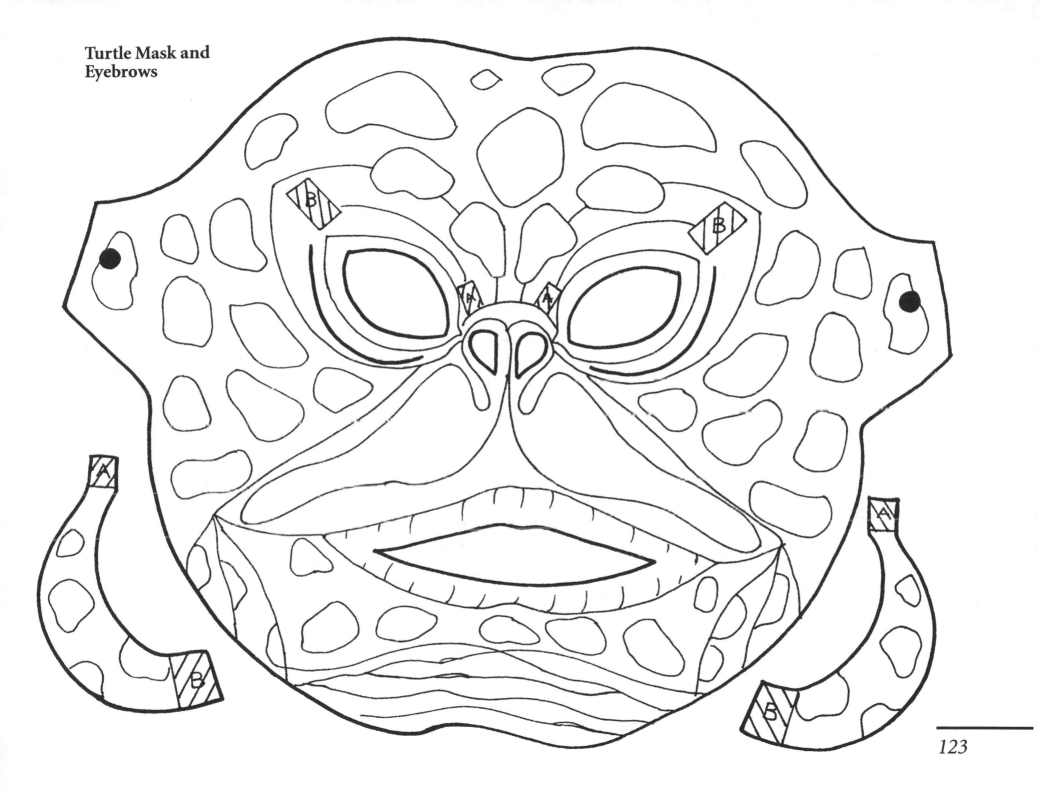

Turtle Breastplate

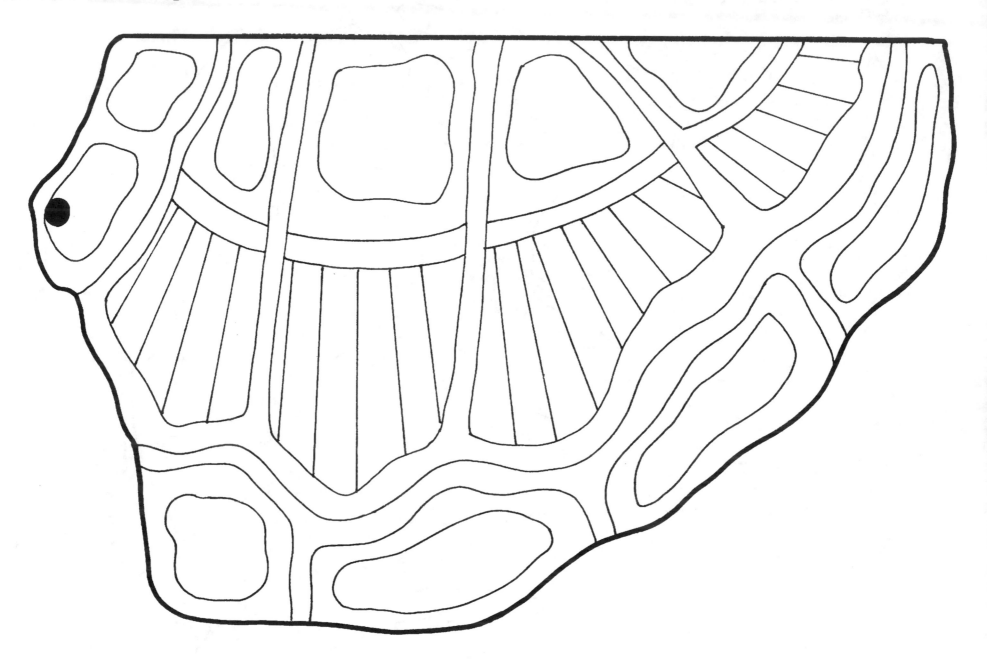

Turtle Breastplate

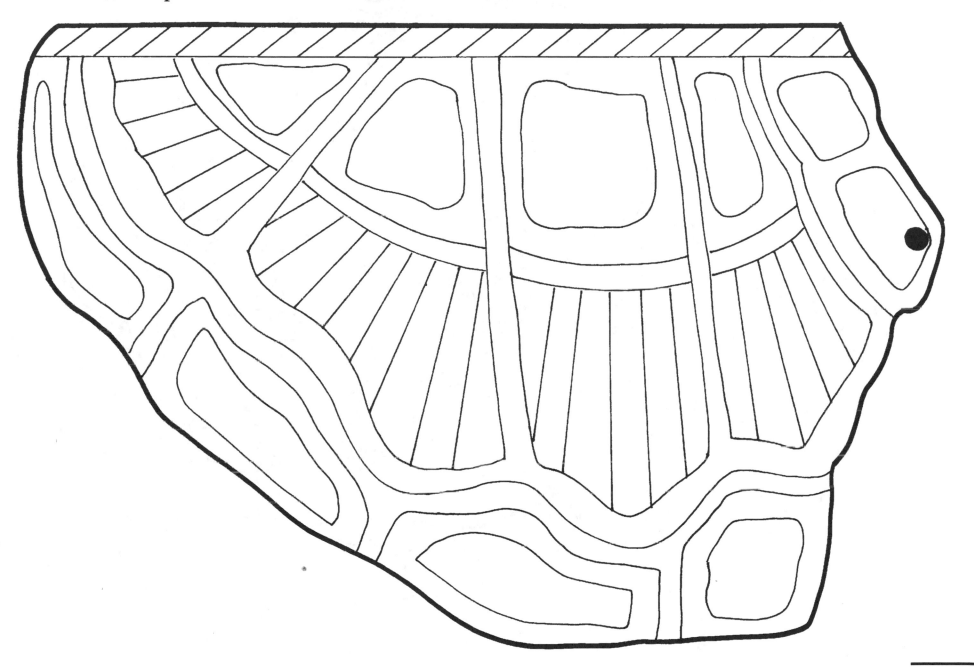

Fish Mask

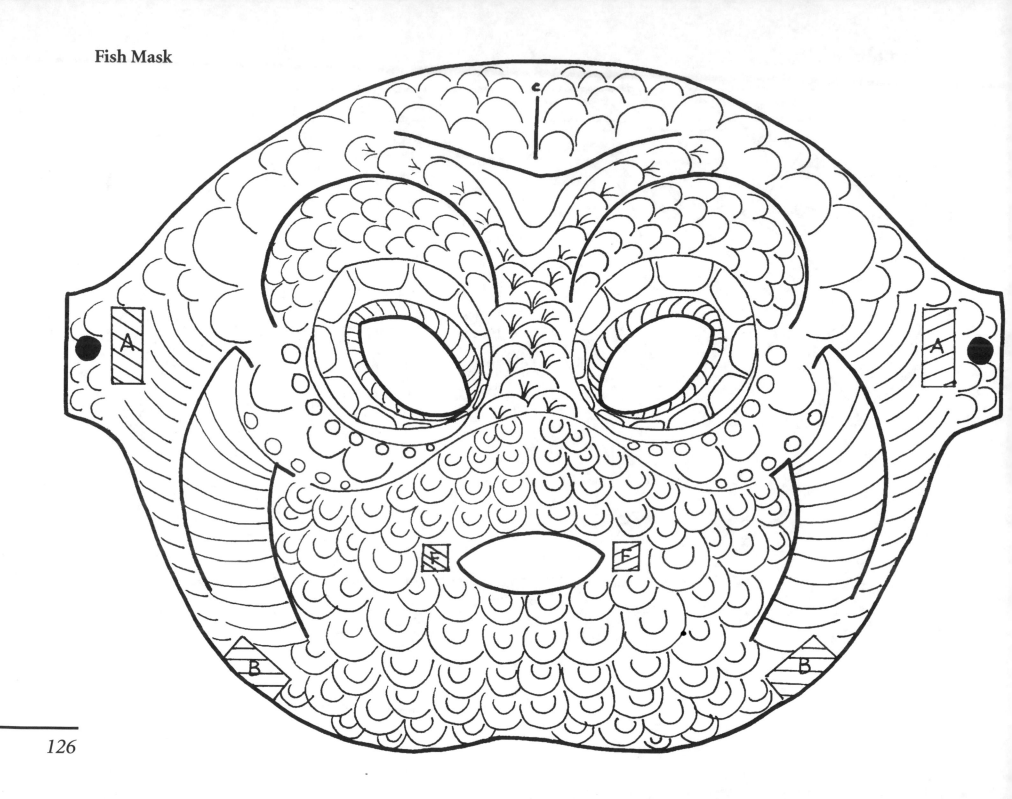

Fish Fins

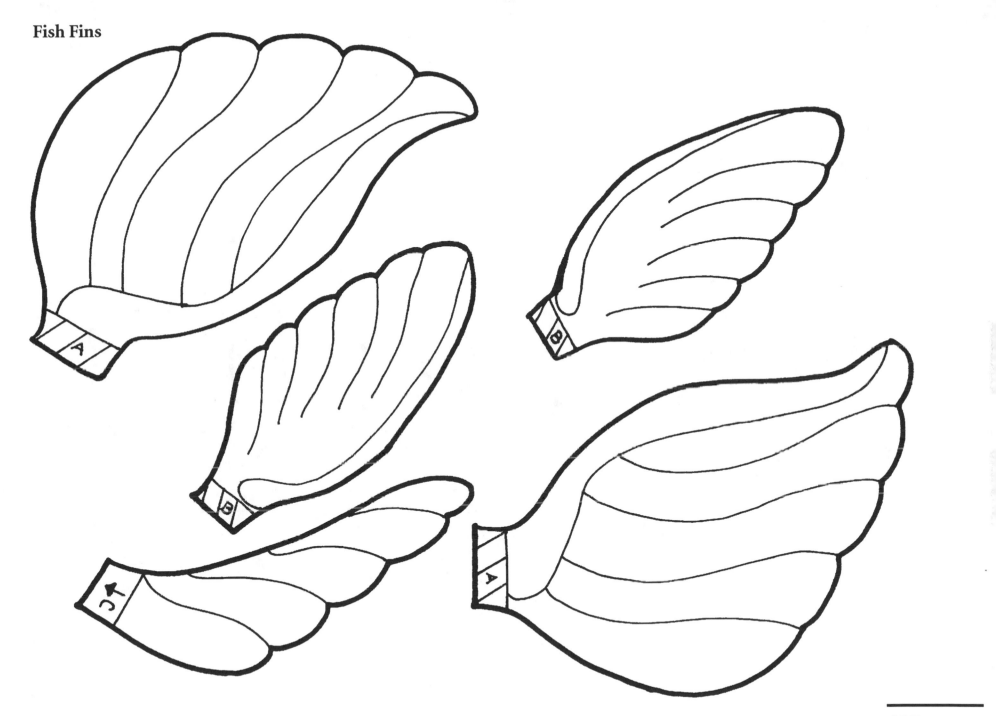

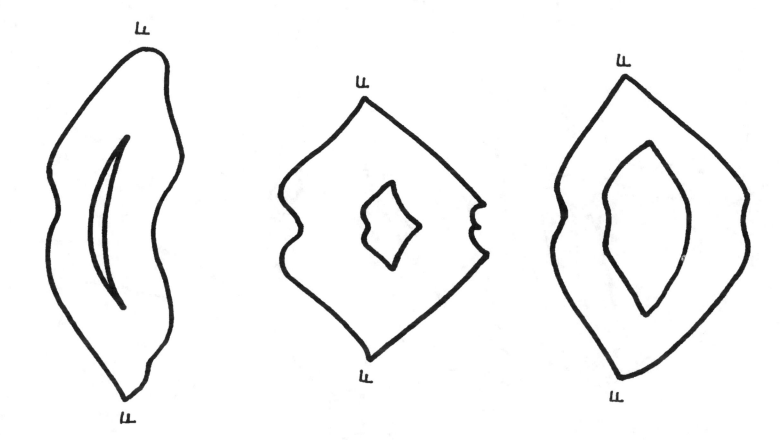

Fish Breastplate

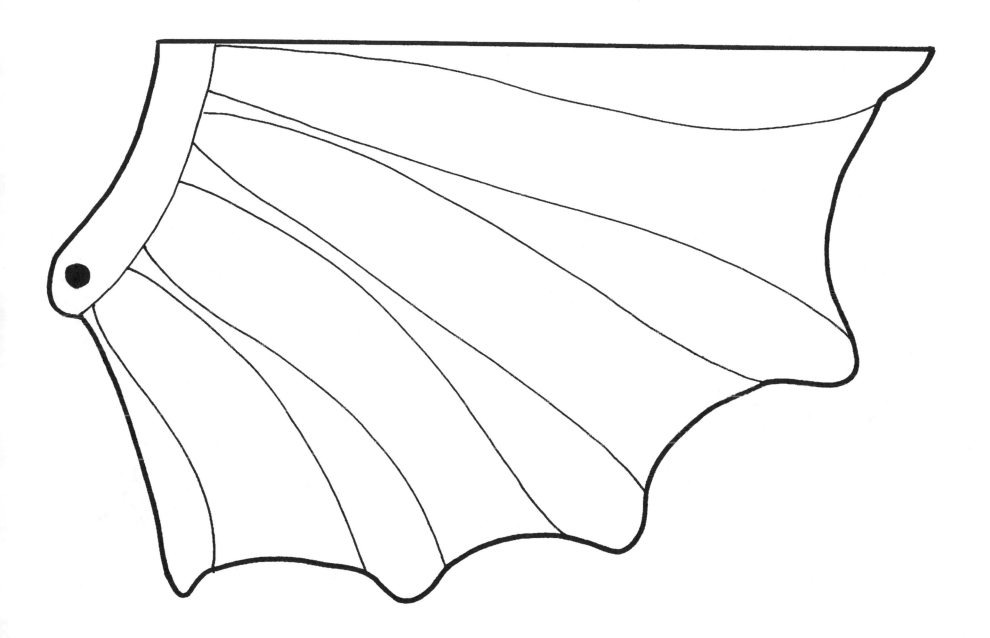

Fish Breastplate

Activities

Listening to a Korean Folk Tale

Background Information

As with many cultures, Korea's relationship with other parts of the world is reflected in its folk tales. The Korean folk tale on which this play is based is similar to the Indian folk tale, "The Gharial and the Monkey." India and Korea are not all that distant from one another, so it is easy to see how one or the other of these folk tales might have made the journey between countries. More curious is the similarity between the Korean folk tale "Konjwi and Patjwi" and the story that Europeans and North Americans know as "Cinderella." The Korean version has at its centre a virtuous young woman who is victimized by a wicked stepmother but befriended by various magical birds and animals and fairies who help her defeat the stepmother's tortures whenever they can. "Konjwi and Patjwi" is rich in details specific to Korean culture. The relationship between tales drawn from different cultures is a question that fascinates folklorists and anthropologists, though no one has any easy answers for the intriguing similarities of many of these tales.

Activity

Your group might enjoy listening to the tale of "Konjwi and Patjwi." One version can be found in the following book:

Climo, Shirley. *The Korean Cinderella*. New York: HarperCollins, 1993.

After the reading, discuss with the children the similarities and differences between the Korean tale and Cinderella. You might also want to talk about what the children learned about Korean culture from the tale.

Writing a Puppet Play Script

Background Information

Like most of the cultures from which this book's plays are drawn, Korea has a long tradition of performing mask dramas. Korea has another popular dramatic tradition—the puppet play. Unlike the mask dramas, which were historically performed by Korean villagers to celebrate things like the harvest moon, puppet plays were performed by professionals. The history of these professional travelling players—the *Kut-chung-p'ae* or *Namsadang*—provides another example of how Korea's geography has resulted in it being influenced by, and in turn influencing, the cultures of neighbouring countries: it is believed that the *Namsadang* came originally from northwest India, migrated through China into Korea, and from Korea eventually journeyed to Japan.

Korean puppet plays make use of three kinds of puppets—marionettes, rod puppets, and glove puppets. Scripts are an important element of Korean puppet plays though they are of minimal importance to Korean mask dramas, which are largely made up of dance, music, and pantomime and are only occasionally interspersed with a line of dialogue—just enough to keep the story moving along! The puppet plays are mostly comic, and like the mask dramas, they often satirize figures like the Buddhist monk and government officials. The puppets are made to move to the rhythm of the play's dialogue and songs.

Activity

Your group may like to mount its own Korean puppet play. The children could start by reading Korean folk tales (see bibliography in "About the Play" for titles) and choosing one to perform.

To write a script for the play, your group will need to decide which characters they need, what the story's key scenes are, and what speeches or lines of dialogue are essential. A Korean puppet play always has a puppet-narrator who explains parts of the story that are not dramatized. After establishing the play's structure by deciding what speeches the puppet-narrator needs to make, your group could break into smaller groups, and each group could tackle writing one of the scenes between the puppet-narrator's speeches. Your group should read the parts aloud to make sure the play works as a whole before embarking upon the challenge (and fun) of matching the words to puppet actions.

Glove and rod puppets are both relatively easy to make. You could use a sock as the base for the puppet, and sew, glue, pin, tape, or staple bits of coloured fabric or felt to the sock to give it facial features and costume it like a character. The children may need to do some research to create authentic costumes. If you would like to create more advanced puppets, consult one of the many books on puppets and puppet-making.

Exploring Calligraphy

Background Information

Calligraphy is Korea's most revered art form. It has been practised in Korea since at least the fifth century B.C.E., but very few pieces from before the sixteenth century have survived the many invasions of Korea. While Korea's mask dramas are a folk art form and have always been performed in every Korean village, up until this century calligraphy was considered an artistocratic art form. Korea's most famous historical calligraphers, Han-Ho, Kim Ku, and Yang Sa-on, were court artists whose work was commissioned by monarchs. As part of their duties at court, these artists trained princes and nobles in their art. Calligraphy was regarded as an ideal way of teaching discipline and noble virtues because it requires a great deal of dedication and patience.

Korean calligraphy uses Chinese characters. The Korean alphabet was not invented until the fifteenth century, by which time the calligraphic tradition was so well established that its use of Chinese characters remained unchanged. The Chinese characters of Korean calligraphy are painted with Indian ink and weasel-tail brushes, sometimes on paper and sometimes on silk. The Chinese characters are ideograms—picture words—and even the smallest dot or stroke on each has a particular significance. Korean calligraphic masters pride themselves on being able to create infinite variations on each Chinese character by altering tiny details of the character to make each drawing of them unique. The difficulty of this is increased by the rules of the art, which forbid the artist from retouching a stroke once the brush has been lifted from the paper or silk. It is the very difficulty of the art that is regarded as its greatest virtue; calligraphy is believed to be one means of obtaining spiritual enlightenment.

Calligraphic art is hung on walls, just like paintings are, so that the skill of the artist can be admired. In fact, Korean calligraphy has had a great influence on the art of Korean painting, which also uses dark, bold strokes for its stylized simplicity.

Activity

To help your group appreciate the art of calligraphy, show them some examples of calligraphic art in books or actual art, if possible. The children could then try creating their own Chinese characters with black paint and fine brushes on white paper. There are many books on calligraphy that they could use as guides, or there may be someone in your community who could come in and instruct the group.

Creating a Sea Collage

Your group might like to create a sea collage that can also be used as a backdrop for their performance of "The Hare's Liver." In preparation, they could conduct research to find out what kind of marine life is found in the waters around the Korean peninsula, then break them into smaller groups, with each group responsible for one panel of the collage.

Use heavy paper for the background (light blue or grey construction paper works well). Children can use a variety of materials to draw and colour their animals, such as felt pens, charcoal, and tempera paint. They can also cut pictures out of magazines or make the animals from coloured paper or tissue paper and then glue them on to the background. Three-dimensional effects can be achieved by adding paper fins, gills, or tentacles. Real rocks and shells can also be added.